Praise for Top Tasks

"The Top Tasks research has shown us that people buy a car the same way throughout Europe, and that the same things matter to them. We learned that people could not find what they were looking for on our website. Due to a very complex product set up, which is common in automotive, we have been struggling for years on how best to present our products to the customers. Through the specific Top Tasks methodology, we finally found a way that allows customers to fulfil their tasks on the Toyota website. A real breakthrough for the industry!"

Tineke Vanmaele, Manager, Digital Experience, Toyota

"We are HUGE advocates of the Top Task methodology at our company and evangelize it to everyone we talk with—both internally and externally. It's really helped us fight against some of the 'bright shiny object' disease and the tendency for everyone to have an opinion of what we put on our web pages."

Jeanne Quinn, Sr. Mgr., Digital & Social Experience, Global Partner Marketing, Cisco

"We used Top Tasks successfully for three software divisions at IBM. It gave us true insight into what visitors wanted to achieve and, just as importantly, what was of less interest. It helped us bring the voice of the customer to the decision table."

John Blackmore, Global Content Marketing, IBM Digital Business Group

"Top Tasks Management is a quick, useful method that has proven itself once and again for stakeholders in Google Search. The pattern that emerges every single time is nothing but powerful and amazing."

Tomer Sharon, Former Senior User Research, Google Search

"What do our customers come to do on our site? Great question. It's surprising how many different answers/opinions you'll hear. At Microsoft, I have used Top Tasks with incredible success—often increasing conversion rates by more than 100% while improving customer satisfaction. Use Top Tasks and get real results, fast."

Peter Horsman, Senior Digital Marketing Lead, Microsoft Cloud + AI

"Inspired by Gerry, I've been using the Top Tasks technique for over ten years in support of the University of Edinburgh's web management community. It's a relatively simple and inexpensive source of user insight, and for me, a valuable route to understanding user priorities."

Neil Allison, User Experience Manager, The University of Edinburgh

"The Top Tasks methodology delivers an unparalleled glimpse into the minds of customers, even for organizations that are skeptical of user research. Top Tasks combines both quantitative and qualitative insights to provide a holistic view of your audience. The outcomes are clear. And your products improve because of them."

Nyckie Pineau, Principal Designer, NetApp

"The Top Task approach has helped us to understand what is important to our patients and service users and start designing digital services that meet their needs. It provides the data and evidence needed to make informed decisions that benefit users."

Ben Cloney, HSE, Acting Head of Digital, Health Service Executive (HSE), Ireland

"We have used Top Tasks for over 10 years, and the philosophy and set of methods have been vital to our clients' digital success. The beauty of Top Tasks is that the whole team gets first-hand knowledge about the customers' needs through prioritized tasks and not the usual vague and misleading hypotheses about what the customer wants."

Jostein Magnussen, Co-Founder Netlife Design, Norway

"Organizations will have to be truly customer obsessed to survive. By using Top Tasks, we help our clients to see what really matters the most. With a fact-driven and inclusive approach, Top Tasks management delivers the necessary tools to navigate clearly in this transformative age. It is always amazing to experience how the Top Task process brings people together and gives them the excitement to focus on what is important. And the excitement only increases once the improved business results are coming in."

David De Block, Managing Partner & Strategist, Internet Architects

"The Top Tasks survey that we undertook with Gerry McGovern revealed interesting insights into what users expect from our website. As a result, we made changes and launched new services to meet our users' needs. The survey results became a valuable management tool for decisions on the long-term direction of the website, and it helped create a common understanding of what the website should and should not be."

Andrea Stojanov, Principal Communications Specialist, Asian Development Bank

"In the first six months since prioritizing top tasks of majors and programs, we've seen an increase in application starts and requests for information."

Jason Buzzell, Director of Digital Communications, University of Nebraska at Omaha

"For over a decade, Top Tasks has been my working method to help clients in Sweden with websites, intranets, and extranets. If I were to summarize Top Tasks with one word, that word would be 'simplicity.' For a group of people that are important to you, you get a list of the most important things you need to help them do. That's basically it. Sure, we all dig into the specifics, we elaborate, sketch and come to conclusions. But at the end of the day—it's a list. And a list is easy to understand. Everyone can relate to it, and even if it sometimes sparks almost existential discussions, it has a better chance of actually affecting decisions than complicated maps or long reports. A thorough process leading to a simple and actionable result: that is, in essence, Top Tasks management."

Fredrik Wackå, Founder, Webbrådgivaren Sverige AB

"From working with clients in government, industry, and higher education for many years, we've found the Top Tasks framework to be a powerful tool that helps managers grow their organization's empathy for customers, backed up by hard-nosed metrics of customers' needs and behaviors."

Mike Atyeo, Co-Founder, Neo Insight

"The logic underpinning Top Tasks management is simple: Get clear evidence of what the priority tasks are for your users, design for achieving those, and measure and improve iteratively. This simplicity is powerful enough to win over the internal agendas, distractions, and barriers that can make a website, intranet, or software far less effective for users and the organization. We've had the pleasure of shining the light of Top Tasks logic onto some complex organizations, and the benefit has been significant and greatly appreciated by our clients."

Chris Rourke, Founder, User Vision

"We've successfully used the Top Tasks method to identify what's important to organizations' customers, be they a government agency's citizens, a social housing association's tenants, a university's students, a hospital's patients and medical specialists, or any type of business's employees. Top Tasks identification more often than not contained a number of surprises regarding what the organization should focus on to really service their customers. And those tasks then proved to be a success when implemented on the organisation's website, intranet, or other digital platform."

Christiaan W. Lustig, Lead Consultant & Managing Partner, Brayton House

"I've found Gerry's Top Task methodology useful both practically and politically. Prioritizing tasks from a customer perspective identifies the best way to spend time and effort. Convincingly communicating customers' priorities to senior stakeholders gets buy-in and removes roadblocks."

Gerry Gaffney, Director and Senior Consultant, Information and Design

"There's something beautiful about Top Tasks that goes beyond the clear and concise nature of the data. Its superpower is found in its ability to help redefine the vision and realignment of an organization to refocus on delivering what truly matters to the people who use a service."

Gerry Scullion, Founder and Director of This is HCD

"For me, Top Tasks are a great tool to improve the digital maturity of organizations. They provide a clear and effective method for the continuous optimization of any digital customer- or employee-facing process. The practicality of the method really helps with explaining to both professionals and management what it's all about and how it can help improve the business."

Erik M. Hartman, Founder, The Information Management Foundation

"What I find rewarding about Top Tasks management is the energy and insights we gain by collaborating with people in organizations in gathering the longlist. It is the process that counts, and working in this way assures that people understand and accept the results. In Top Tasks management, I see a way of making great websites that work, and that really is the best publicity an organization can get."

Wiep Hamstra, Owner, De Staat van het Web, The Netherlands

"We had the privilege of working with Gerry at the OECD. Without the evidence we collected from the Top Tasks process, we would never have been able to get a real grasp of our audience needs."

Cynthia Coutu, Former Head of Internet Unit, OECD

"Top Tasks are the basis for everything we do in our work on Canada.ca. We adopted the framework early on when developing Canada.ca's IA and navigation so we could optimize findability. We use Top Tasks to decide which content problems to tackle first, and for benchmarking usability performance. It's really given us a clear model for how to prioritize where we direct our energy in managing Canada.ca."

Peter Smith, Chief, Canada.ca Product Design, Treasury Board of Canada Secretariat

"A major Top Tasks survey of the European Commission's online presence was carried out in 2014. The goal of the survey was to find out the main reasons why people want to interact with our organization. It was in 24 languages and ran across 28 countries."

European Commission

"We've been working to formulate a process for government to define Top Tasks alongside Gerry McGovern, an expert on digital user experience and developer of the Top Tasks management model."

Katie Taylor, User Research Lead, GOV.UK

"Organizing and optimizing our Canada Revenue Agency site by Top Tasks instead of by audience has shown an increase in findability by 93% and task success by 115%."

Jonathan Rath, Manager, Web Services Section, Canada Revenue Agency

"Few UX methods offer more quick insights than a top tasks analysis. This deceptively simple method should be one of the first things every product team does to know what users want to do with a website, app or product."

Jeff Sauro, PHD, Founding Principal, MeasuringU

First edition

Published in 2018

Silver Beach Publishing
Silver Beach
Gormanston
Meath
Ireland
K32 YN40

ISBN: 978-1-9164446-0-7
Cover Design & Layout: Lisa Coffey
Editing: Rosilda Moreira Alves McGovern, Alexander Spring

www.customercarewords.com

Top Tasks

How to identify, measure and improve customer top tasks

For Rosilda

CONTENTS

Why Top Tasks?   **13**

Why Top Tasks?. 15

Top Tasks Identification. **23**

Defining scope 25

Gathering tasks. 28

Shortlisting: getting to your final list. 42

Designing the survey 65

Encouraging people to vote 75

Analyzing and presenting results 77

Customer Architecture. **87**

Seven principles of effective digital navigation . . . 89

Designing a customer architecture 101

Task Performance Indicator. **127**

Customer success and time 129

Creating task instructions 141

Measuring. 153

Analyzing, presenting, using results 167

1

Why Top Tasks?

Why Top Tasks?

Top tasks are what matter most to your customers. By identifying and continuously improving top tasks you will deliver a better customer experience and increased organizational value.

People are more powerful, skeptical, and impatient today than they've ever been. They want what they want *now* through the device they have at hand now. People are extremely demanding these days, and it's only going to get worse.

This changes the relationship between the organization and the customer. Do you remember that thing called "control?" It used to be that organizations had a lot of control over the customer. The product didn't need to be that fantastic as long as you had fantastic marketing and advertising. If you worked for the government, then citizens just had to accept what they were given. And if the interface was clunky and unintuitive, then they always had the manual or the support staff. That world is fading.

Organizations need to make things simple today, really simple. They need to understand the customer/user much better. The design of their products must be genuinely intuitive—so simple even a distracted adult can understand it.

The truth is that organizations love complexity, verbosity, and glut. Giving a website to an organization is like giving a pub to an alcoholic. Every hour is Happy Hour as they publish, publish, publish. Designing apps is pretty much the same, as 'featuritis' spreads rapidly. Typically, when organizations delete up to 90 percent of what they have, everything begins to work much better. Yeah, I'm serious. Totally, totally serious.

- The Norwegian Cancer Society reduced their website size from 4,000 down to 1,000 pages. Donations and satisfaction rose substantially as a result.
- Liverpool City went from 4,000 pages to 700 and saw lots of positive results.
- Telenor Norway went from 4,000 to 500 pages. Sales and customer satisfaction went up. Customer support inquiries went down.
- The UK National Trust reduced their web presence from 50,000 to 9,000.
- The U.S Department of Health deleted 150,000 out of 200,000 pages. Nobody noticed.

What? Why? Because organizations excel at creating vast quantities of useless stuff. What matters most to the organization often matters least to the customer. In a great many organizations we have worked for we have found an inverse relationship between the importance of something to customers and the amount of effort the organization was putting into it. Crazy, isn't it? But I'm sure you know what I'm talking about.

It's those damn tiny tasks! When a tiny task goes to sleep at night, it dreams of being a top task. And when it wakes up it is full of ambition and ego. Lots of digital teams are being nibbled to death by a deluge of tiny organizational tasks that will clutter an interface and clog a search. They will drain vital resources away from the continuous effort required to make customer top tasks simpler and better.

Top Tasks helps you fight ego with evidence—evidence of what customer top tasks are and how these tasks are performing. Evidence of what the real customer experience is like.

What Top Tasks does for you

Top Tasks is a way of managing the online customer experience by understanding and improving what matters most to customers. It is based on the following principles:

- That the most important thing to a customer when they are online is the task they want to complete.
- That in any environment or general activity (health, buying a car, choosing a university, etc.) there are top tasks. There are roughly ten top tasks in any particular environment.
- That organizational goals will be reached more easily and quickly when customer top tasks are well-served.
- That we can reliably identify these top tasks with clear data and evidence.
- That we can reliably measure how successful customers are at completing these top tasks, and how long it is taking them.
- That we can build a highly intuitive information architecture based on top tasks data.
- That if we focus on an ongoing basis on increasing success rates and reducing time-on-task for these top tasks we will deliver an excellent customer experience.

Top Tasks has been developed as a result of 15 years of research and practice. It has been used in more than 30 countries and languages. Over 300,000 people have participated. Large organizations such as Cisco, Toyota,

Microsoft, IBM, European Union, Tetra Pak, the BBC, and Google have successfully used Top Tasks. It has been used a great many times by small and medium municipalities, universities, intranets, associations, and businesses in countries such as Norway, Sweden, Holland, Belgium, the United Kingdom, Canada, and the United States. It's been road-tested. It works.

Is Top Tasks right for you?

The more times you answer "Yes" to the following questions, the more likely Top Tasks is to benefit your organization:

1. Do you have a large, complex website or app and have the feeling that things are getting out-of-control?
2. Is there internal disagreement as to who your customers are and what they really want to do?
3. Is there a lack of empathy for and understanding of your customers' top tasks within your organization?
4. Is there a lack of quality customer data available?
5. Is the focus of digital strategy on potential customers, with current customers being neglected?
6. Is there a lack of interaction with and observation of customers?
7. Are content and apps making things hard to find and hard to navigate?
8. Is much of this content and apps out-of-date?
9. Is there rapid, out-of-control growth of content and apps?
10. Is there low customer demand for much of this stuff?
11. Is much of the content and apps of low quality?
12. Are things very 'silo'-driven, with a lack of cross-organizational collaboration and cooperation?
13. Is it a launch-and-leave culture driven by projects and campaigns, rather than one of continuous improvement?
14. Are decisions generally based on opinion, politics, and ego?
15. Does the organization like to communicate at the customer, rather than truly listen to them?

The more you have answered 'yes' to the above questions, the more potential Top Tasks has to benefit your organization — potential — because you need to answer 'yes' to the following two questions as well:

1. Does management recognize it has a problem?

2. Do they want to make the effort to change?

Is there a genuine desire within your organization to transform and become more customer-centric? Do they really want to deliver a great and genuine customer experience? Is there a true desire to change the culture? Are they driven to become:

- Customer-obsessed
- Evidence-based
- Continuously improving
- Silo-bridging
- Simple and clear
- Transparent and open

Because that's what customers are expecting of organizations these days. It is the customer who is setting the agenda. It is the customer who feels in control. That's the shift. From organization-centric to customer-centric. And Top Tasks is designed to get you right into the center of the world of the customer. To understand what matters most to them (their top tasks), and to be able to continuously improve these top tasks by increasing their success rates and reducing the time it takes to complete them.

Top Tasks allows you to stand in the shoes of your customers, to see the world as they see it, to feel the pain and frustration that they feel. You will have statistically reliable evidence. You will be able to say:

- These are the customers' top tasks.
- Here's how they're performing.
- Here's what we need to do to make things better.

Top Tasks works whether you provide content, software, websites, or apps. It works for employees in intranets and digital workplaces, as well as for customers and citizens. Wherever you've got complexity and politics, Top Tasks can give you a clear path forward to deliver a truly excellent customer experience.

Who Top Tasks is less well suited for

1. For immature digital environments (websites, apps), where customer experience is not really taken seriously by management, who instead

demand cliché images, brochureware, and who think they can control the message and the journey of the customer.

2. For traditional 'brand' heavy organizations, where the brand is low on information but high on image and emotion. Top Tasks works much better for a Cisco than it does for a Coca-Cola, for example.
3. For traditional, hierarchical, ego-driven organizations.
4. For organizations that are very distant from their customers and where it is very difficult to get in touch with customers.
5. For very small websites and apps with only a few pages and small customer bases.

Ongoing management metric

Top Tasks is designed to be an ongoing management model for managing the customer experience. It is made up of:

1. Top tasks identification
2. Customer architecture design
3. Task Performance Indicator (TPI)

Task identification involves finding out what matters most (top tasks) and what matters least (tiny tasks) to customers. It involves:

1. Collecting a list of all possible tasks that customers may want to complete.
2. Refining this list until it is between 50 and 100 tasks.
3. Getting in the region of 400 customers to vote on this list and choose their top tasks.
4. Creating a task league table from the results; from the top tasks (the most voted for) to the tiny tasks (the least voted for).

A customer architecture gives you the foundations for highly-intuitive navigation. It involves:

1. Getting about 15 customers to rank the top 30 or so tasks from the task identification vote.
2. Developing a hypothetical classification from this ranking.
3. Getting more customers to test this classification by giving them about 30 task instructions.
4. Refining this classification over the course of three phases until it achieves at least an 80% success rate.

The Task Performance Indicator (TPI) is about giving you reliable, defensible success and time metrics for customer top tasks. It allows you to say: "This task has a 40% failure rate and even those who succeed at completing it are taking four times too long to complete it." It involves:

1. Selecting the 8-12 top tasks for measurement, based on the task identification voting results.
2. Developing task instructions for each of these top tasks.
3. Selecting 13-18 customers who will be asked to try and complete these task instructions on the website or app in question.
4. Carrying out the measurements with these customers in a moderated way, using a remote meeting service such as GoToMeeting or WebEx. Recording audio and the screen of each customer being observed.
5. Carefully moderating each measurement session with the objective of:
   a. Ensuring that each participant clearly understands each task instruction and what they are expected to try and do;
   b. Creating as natural and realistic an environment as possible; one that allows the participant to focus on the task itself with as little distraction as possible;
   c. Clearly identifying task success rates and time spent on the task;
   d. Identifying the key causes of task failure and slow completion times.
6. Coming up with clear recommendations that will reduce failure and time-on-task.
7. Reporting results to management. Drawing up plans for changes based on what has been observed, making those changes, measuring and reporting again and again and again. (TPI is a management model and an ongoing process, not a project.)

While reliable metrics of the customers' actual experience are a key deliverable of the TPI, perhaps its most important deliverable is the ongoing empathy, understanding, and insight it allows us into the customer experience. The biggest thing missing today in most organizations is empathy for the customer. The number one reason for this lack of empathy is that employees, who are creating content, code, visuals, for customers, rarely actually see customers using their work.

The TPI is typically run on a six-monthly or yearly basis. It is not meant to be the only observation of customers done by any means. Its purpose is to give solid management figures of customer task performance, and by extension, the customer experience. In between TPI measurements, you can run scaled-down versions of the TPI, or standard usability testing, A/B testing and/or data analytics. In fact, it is advised that not a week should go by without observation of customer behavior. It's all about managing based on what customers are actually doing.

The TPI will allow you to make statements such as:

- 40 percent of customers are failing to complete their top tasks. Those who do succeed are taking an average of four minutes longer than they should.
- Since the last TPI, we made specific changes. These changes have resulted in a ten percent overall increase in the success rate. Time-on-task has been reduced by an average of 15 seconds.
- We predict that if we make the following changes, we will see an average of a five percent increase in the task success rate, and an average of a ten-second reduction in time-on-task.

It's essential that you are measuring and continuously improving top tasks. If you measure and then improve tiny tasks (low demand tasks), then you may well make the overall customer experience worse. Why? Because to improve a tiny task:

- You may make it easier to find in the navigation by, for example, adding more links about this task. That can distract from the links for the top tasks. It essentially creates clutter.
- You may make it more findable through search functions. Optimizing tiny tasks in search functions nearly always has a negative impact on top task 'findability' through search functions.
- You may create more features or content for it — that means more stuff for your customers to wade through as they try and complete their top tasks. It's more stuff for you to manage — a great many teams spend their time creating new features and content for tiny tasks, instead of continuously improving top task content.

In summary, Top Tasks Management allows you to:

1. Clearly identify the top and tiny tasks your customers are seeking to complete.
2. Design an intuitive classification for your customers.

3. Accurately measure completion rates and times for the top tasks.
4. Identify the causes of task failure and slow completion times.
5. Make changes.
6. Measure again. Did the changes work? How can success rates be improved even further? How can time-on-task be reduced even more?
7. Continuously measure and improve, measure and improve, measure and improve those customer top tasks.

2

Top Tasks Identification

Defining scope

Top Tasks Identification will identify, in a statistically defensible manner, the top tasks and tiny tasks of your customers. To get started you must answer these two questions:

1. Who will be asked to vote?
2. What is the task environment?

In an intranet, it might be easy to decide that all staff should be able to vote. In a business, getting current and potential customers to vote would be an obvious first step. But what about partners and suppliers? Should they be allowed to vote as well? And what about job seekers? Generally, we would recommend avoiding mixing job seekers and potential and current customers, because they have quite different tasks. So, we'd have a Top Tasks identification for current and potential customers, and then, if required, a separate one for job seekers.

Try and keep the scope within the world of the customer. So, for a health organization, try and frame the scope as 'all tasks that someone might interest a visitor which are connected with their health.' We advise against limiting the scope to a particular website or app because:

1. It immediately introduces an organization-centric view of the world, rather than a customer-centric one.
2. It limits the ability of the digital environment to grow and evolve. Let's say the organization doesn't deal with task X. If we discover that task X is the fifth top task for customers, then the organization gets valuable insight. They now can plan to develop content/tools for task X.

In fact, you even should avoid framing things from a digital perspective. "Buying a car"; "Choosing a university"; "Dealing with health": these are all better ways to frame tasks. Remember, people don't think in digital or physical terms. They think: "I'd love to visit Paris"; "What is this pain in my side?"; "I need to buy a new computer." The core of Top Tasks is to think like a customer.

Be prepared to spend time deciding on the target audience and scope, because the decisions you make here will frame how you move forward. Involve as many departments/units of your organization as possible. This is key. This is crucial. If you start making decisions about what the scope and tasks are from one department's perspective, the result will be skewed according to that department's perspective. As a result, it will be difficult to get other departments to accept and act on the results.

Who should be involved?

- A typical Top Tasks stakeholder group will consist of between three and eight people.
- These people need to be experienced and to come from all the major stakeholder groups within the organization.
  - For an intranet: Communications, IT, HR, Support, Products, Services, Finance, Marketing, Sales departments.
  - For a public website/app: Marketing, Sales, Support, Products, Services departments.
- It is of great importance to have people from different departments and with different perspectives. In many organizations, people work in silos. In really big organizations, they hardly know each other. During the Top Tasks sessions, it often happens that they find out that they are in fact working on the same tasks, that they are duplicating content, and that they have a lot in common. They will also probably find that they are using different jargon for the same thing. Encourage and cherish these conversations, organize your meetings in a manner whereby they will have time to talk to each other. They help for working towards a buy-in and provide a basis for future cooperation inside the organization.
- The more stakeholders there are, the more likely you are to get an accurate list of tasks. When the stakeholders are from different departments, they start becoming a check on each other. If, for example, one person wants a frivolous task included, someone from another department will likely speak up. This helps eliminate the 'ego-driven' tasks and get a good balance on the final list of tasks.
- You are the conductor—hence, the voice of the customer. You are constantly feeding the stakeholders with customer data: what they're doing, what they're saying, where they're visiting, what the top support calls are, some recent survey data, how our competitors name a certain task.
- Those you select need to be able to commit to the entire process. It will make everything much longer and more frustrating for all involved if people are dropping in and out of the sessions. The new people joining will need to be educated about the process. They are unlikely to understand it

immediately and will start asking what seem to everyone else to be fairly obvious questions. They will probably start asking about tasks that you will have already deleted. This will lead to frustration and annoyance on behalf of those who have been present from the beginning.

- If you identify some crucial stakeholders who clearly will not have time to attend all sessions, then wait until near the very end of the task short-listing process, and then ask them to review the final list.

Gathering tasks

What is a task?

A task is whatever your customer wants to do. So, "pricing" is a task, "configuration" is a task, "parking" is a task. How is it best to describe a task? This is something we shall discuss in further detail later on. However, here are some quick tips.

Verbs should be avoided: words like "find" or "get" are simply too vague, and they make tasks hard to scan-read — which is how people tend to read online. You should only use verbs when you absolutely have to. For example, if you refer to "symptoms", this may not be explicit enough on its own, and you may have to write "check symptoms". Remember, you are always trying to capture the essence of what your customer wants to do.

Working with information is a task. Absolutely. Totally. For sure. Some have the mistaken assumption that a task is only something you do with a tool/app. This is simply not true. Everything the customer wants to do is a task. If they want to see if they qualify for something, then that's a task. If they want to compare two products, that's a task. If they want to configure, install, troubleshoot, get an overview, read a detailed specification—these are all tasks.

What is not a task?

- 'Searching' is not a task. What are they searching for?
- 'Navigating' is not a task. What are they navigating for?
- 'Clicking' is not a task. Why are they clicking?
- 'Logging in' is generally not a task. Why are they logging in? Do they want to transfer money, check a balance, etc.?

Building the task list

When you're building the task list, you are doing two things: one which is obvious, one which is not so obvious. The obvious aspect is that you are collecting customer tasks. The less obvious aspect is that you are changing the organization, making it more customer-centric.

If you're in the lucky five percent of organizations that are truly, genuinely customer-centric, then you don't need to worry about changing the organization. You can just focus on collecting the tasks.

If you are part of the other 95%, then you will need to use the task collection process as a way to reach out to key stakeholders and explain that being truly customer-centric means focusing on helping customers complete their top tasks as quickly and simply as possible.

The process of figuring out what customers want most and relentlessly making it easier and faster for them to do these things may seem blindingly obvious to you. However, you may be surprised to discover that it is not so blindingly obvious to many of your fellow employees. In fact, to many, it is wholly counter-intuitive. Many people, particularly within larger organizations struggle to have any concept of who their customers are, let alone to have an understanding of the tasks customers want to complete and desire to help them quickly and easily complete these tasks. This is radical stuff.

Treat this as your opportunity to reach out to as many parts of the organization as possible and evangelize the benefits of a great customer experience. Collecting the customer tasks is your excuse to make contacts, build bridges, and change hearts and minds. The effort that you and your team make to reach out will directly affect the chances of the Top Tasks results being accepted and acted on by the various parts of the organization.

There are two steps involved in building your task list:

1. Gathering potential tasks.
2. Refining and reaching a final list of tasks.

Collection of tasks

Use a spreadsheet. At this stage, the most important thing is to collect the tasks. No matter how rough your description of them may seem, just keep adding them to column A in the spreadsheet. It's important to avoid editing at this stage of the process. You need to be able to show your raw sources. Remember, you are gathering evidence. You may well need to prove at every step of the way that you were as objective and evidence-based as possible.

Tasks

Access to finance

access to law and justice for poor people

access to law justice and human rights for poor people

access to lawyer

active farmer (definition)

Activity report 2010

Advice on what Master studies are recognised in the EU

agenda for the July 21 Summit

agriculture grant

aid delivery methods

Alarm number Europe

Animal Protection

animal rights

Annex 2

Annual accounts

This is a tiny sample of more than 2,000 potential tasks collected for the European Commission Top Tasks survey in 2014. Of course, it's all very rough and needs a huge amount of work. But that's ok.

Sources for potential tasks

You need to build a list of potential tasks. There are two core sources for these tasks:

Source	Amount of effort
Customer	80% of effort and tasks
Organization	20% of effort and tasks

Remember, the essence of Top Tasks is to create a truly customer-centric organization. Thus, when you are developing your initial task list, about 80 percent of your list should come from customer sources. Think within the world of your customer. Don't limit tasks to what your organization deals with at the moment. Keep a broad focus. If a task your organization doesn't deal with gets a big vote, that's an indication of an unmet need that must be addressed. However, you should not exclude what the organization thinks, wants, and does. About 20% of the tasks you collect should represent the organization's perspective.

Customer sources for tasks

The following are sources of tasks from the world of the customer:

- Search-data both from external search engines and from your own site search engine.
- Website/app data analysis: most popular sections, pages, downloads, etc.
- Surveys and research on customers going back two to three years.
- Support or other sorts of help requests.
- Social media, blogs, communities, traditional media.
- Competitors/peers (typically four to six).
- A task collection survey that uses an open-ended question to ask people what their top three tasks are. This is a kind of preliminary survey, and is typically used where the other sources are poor or nonexistent.

Search sources

There are two search sources:

a. The organization's search engine
b. Public search engines (such as Google or Bing)

For your own organization's search engine, you should:

a. Get 12 month's worth of data if at all possible, so that you deal with any search seasonality issues. For example, maybe certain things are searched for a lot during winter but searched for very little during summer.
b. Capture the top 50-100 of these annual searches.

For certain task lists, a service such as Google AdWords can be very useful. When we were doing a Top Tasks identification for the UK National Health Service (NHS), we spent quite a bit of time searching on Google AdWords. Below are search data from Google on the terms "cancer" and "diabetes".

"Cancer" top searches on Google included:

- Stomach cancer
- Lung cancer symptoms
- Bone cancer
- Breast cancer symptoms
- Brain tumor
- Bone cancer
- Testicular cancer
- Throat cancer symptoms

For "diabetes," top searches on Google included:

- Diabetes symptoms
- Symptoms of diabetes
- Diabetes mellitus
- What is diabetes
- Diabetes type 2
- Diabetes diet
- Glucose

As we'll see later, when we are building a health task-list, we don't include the disease/condition itself. Just as if we were compiling a task list for Cisco, we would not include the list of Cisco products. We're looking for a universality for our tasks. "Check symptoms" would be an example of such a universal task: it will be relevant regardless of the disease/condition. "Pricing" is a universal task: it will be relevant regardless of the product type. These are the type of tasks we're looking for.

Have a look at the lists for "cancer" and "diabetes" again, and see if you can identify other universal tasks.

"Diet" and "what is" could be potential universal tasks. But we need to do more research. Why "diet"? Because diet can have an impact on multiple conditions and diseases. At this stage, if in doubt, add it to your list.

Something like Google AdWords is great because it shows the raw, unfiltered search behavior of your customers out there on the Web. It gives you broad insights about general customer behavior rather than behavior which is specific to your current website or app. In building your task list, you want to get into the world of your customers as much as possible, and out of the world of your organization.

Some will say: "Why not just depend on search data?" Searches are just one of many windows through which to view the tasks people want to do. Here are a few reasons for this:

- Experienced, repeat visitors often search less for their top tasks, because they already know how to get there through navigation or bookmarks. When these individuals do a search, they tend to search for more minor, tiny tasks.
- There are certain types of tasks that are never searched for. For example, in a master's university program, we found that an important task was "advancing my career." However, people were not searching with the words "advancing my career".
- With Microsoft Excel, lots of people were searching for "remove conditional formatting." Excel created a page for this task but it always got a lot of negative feedback. When they dug deeper they found that people who were trying to do conditional formatting would often make mistakes, and then search for "remove conditional formatting." That was the trigger. However, the real task was to format properly using conditional formatting. So sometimes, what people search for is not really what they want.
- There may also be times when the environment just doesn't deal with a particular task, and therefore the likelihood of references to that task coming up in searches, particularly if it is a mature environment, can be quite small.
- In websites that historically have had poor search functions, then it is likely that the search data will be poor too, as people avoid using the search function, and only use it as a last resort.
- Where the website has really good navigation, there's a strong chance that important tasks feature significantly in searches, because people can easily find these tasks already using navigation. An extreme example of this behavior happened on the BBC intranet, years ago. On the intranet

homepage, they introduced a section called "Top 10 Searches." Employees began to click on these links and thus stopped searching for them. Six months later, the team noticed that there were a new top ten searches, and so they replaced the old top ten with the new top ten. What happened? The old top ten became the new top ten searches again.

Searches are a good source for researching customer tasks. But it will not be sufficient to identify the actual top tasks of your customers. And remember, the most important thing you're doing is talking, evangelizing, and reaching out within your organization and building consensus about what the customer tasks are.

Website/App Usage Analysis

- Get visitor data on an annual basis if possible, to avoid seasonal variations.
- Typically, all you need to take from this source is the top 50, certainly no more than the top 100.
- Gather data from across the entire digital environment: pages, files, and systems.
- Many of the highest visited pages will likely be sub-homepages, containing a variety of tasks which will need to be unpacked.

Add those tasks to column A in your spreadsheet.

Surveys and research on customers

- Collect tasks from surveys and other customer research that has been carried out in the last two to three years.
- This can include research that your own organization has done or independent research that you have access to.

Support or other sorts of help requests

- Gather the top 50 support requests in the last 12 months.
- Gather the top customer feedback.
- These tend to be very useful sources.

Social media, blogs, communities

- What are the tasks that are cropping up on social media, blogs, and in communities?

- Sometimes, there are vibrant independent communities dedicated to a particular subject. For example, when we did task identification for Microsoft Visual Studio, there was a whole range of independent developer communities, where we were able to gather lots of potential tasks.
- Are there commercial media out there that focus on this particular subject? What are they saying about customer tasks?

Competitors/peers

- Identify the top four to six competitors/peers
- Usually, it's enough to gather tasks from the first couple of levels of their websites/apps.
- You'll begin to see lots of repeated tasks. This is a good sign. You will start to get a sense of the task ecosystem.

Task collection survey

- If you have trouble gathering a comprehensive list of tasks from the above sources (if you have poor search results and analytics data, for example), or if you are dealing with a relatively new environment, then a task collection survey may help.
- This is a very simple survey, usually with just one question: "What are the top three most important things to you …."
- Try and get a couple of hundred customers to take this survey.

Organization sources for tasks

While roughly 80% of the sources should be from the customer, about 20% should be from the organization. These would include:

- Corporate philosophy, strategy, mission, and vision: Make sure that you read up on strategy and various other plans and documents.
- Stakeholder interviews and reviews: You'll want to interview key stakeholders at the beginning of the process, not so much to gather potential tasks, but rather to explain the whole Top Tasks approach. Later, when the task list is nearly finished, you should guide important stakeholders through it to ensure that they are satisfied and approve it.
- Political/Cool: You should consider allocating about five percent of your final list to tasks that you pretty much know the customer doesn't want, but which you do know the organization wants or feels excited about.

It's important that these sorts of tasks are left on the list to demonstrate that they don't get a big vote.

Task collection template

Avoid editing and deleting while initially collecting tasks. You want to be able to show that you were as comprehensive and thorough as possible. Also, where possible, editing and deleting should be a consensual and collaborative process, except for very obvious grammatical issues, direct duplicates, etc.

Your initial 'longlist' might be anything from 150 to 500 tasks. (The European Commission was an exception at 2,000-plus tasks.) The following image shows how we organize the task-list.

Select up to 5 tasks / resources (from the list below) that are MOST IMPORTANT to you when ...							
Tasks	Overlap	Sub-Group	Group	Source	Internal Source	* Del / ?	Notes

Task question wording

- The task question should always be at the top of your list to remind you of the purpose and the context of the tasks below. (See preceding image: "What's most important to you in your day-to-day job?")
- Note down a draft task question as early as you can. It really helps in framing conversations as you go about cleaning up your list.
- Avoid framing the question from the point of view of the organization. Avoid saying things like: "on our website", "while using our app."
- Frame it within the world of your customer: "Select up to five of the tasks/resources from the list below that are *most important* to you in dealing with health ... when buying a car ... when choosing a university ..."

Tasks

This is the column where you place everything you have collected that you think is or can become a task.

Overlap

As you are shortlisting you will use this column where you think two or more tasks are overlapping or are very similar.

Tasks	Overlap
Healthcare in another EU country (incl. when travelling or resident, EU health card, payments and reimbursements, right to treatment)	moving
Moving between EU countries (e.g. implications, work, study, family, healthcare ⋯)	moving
Residence formalities (passport, permanent residence, short stays, card to enter EU, work permits, etc.)	moving
Social security coordination	moving

The preceding four tasks have overlapped and been placed under the subtitle of "moving." (The choice of the overlap title word is not so important.) Clearly, there are some similarities but it will take quite a bit of discussion to ensure these tasks are properly separated and distinct.

Tasks	Overlap	Source
Book your GP appointment online	appointment	patients.co.uk
Let me book an appointment	appointment	user goals doc
Make an appointment	appointment	mayoclinic.com
Remind me when it's time for my appointment	appointment	user goals doc
Request an appointment	appointment	netwellness

- Here the overlap is more obvious. There is one task about booking an appointment and another task about a reminder for an appointment already booked.
- If you look at the "Source" column, you see the reason for the overlap: all of these tasks have come from different sources.
- Should these be two separate tasks, such as "Book an appointment", "Appointment reminder"?
- Or should it just be one task, such as "Appointments (book, remind)"?
- That's a decision to leave until later in the shortlisting process when the list is a lot shorter and more refined. Then, you can have a discussion about whether "appointments" is important enough to have two tasks on the list, or whether one is enough.
- Whatever happens, at the end of your shortlisting process, your "Overlap" column must be blank.

Group/Sub-Group

- This allows you to put your tasks into logical groups so that you can categorize your list while reading it, rather than simply going up and down one long list.
- Don't begin to group tasks until after at least the first shortlisting session with stakeholders. Delete the obvious items and merge them first, otherwise, you will be going to a lot of effort putting group names on tasks that you will soon be deleting.
- Every task must ultimately belong to a group.
- For larger lists of tasks (200–300 or more), you will need both "Group" and "Sub-Group" headings, but for smaller lists, you probably don't need to worry about using a "Sub-Group".
- It's important to avoid spending too much time in naming your "Groups". You need to stress to participants in the shortlisting process that the group names are not an attempt at classification and that they are not intended to be used for navigation design. They might well end up being useful, but if people think that they will definitely be used for classification then lots of time can disappear discussing them. This will make the shortlisting process unnecessarily long. Make sure that the vast majority of the focus during shortlisting is on the tasks themselves (the first column).

Tasks	Overlap	Sub-Group	Group
Application deployment			Develop
Branching and merging			Develop
Bug tracking, trending			Develop
Build management			Develop
Code analysis			Develop
Code profiling			Develop
Writing secure code			Develop
Extend Visual Studio			Develop
Release management			Develop

- A "Group" for Microsoft Developer Technologies (Visual Studio) was called "Develop."
- Groups allow you to segment the list and come at it from a number of different angles. If you're just going up and down one long list all the time, you develop "list-blindness" and begin to miss important things.

Source

- This is where the task came from.
- This is the one column you should fill in immediately when you are entering your tasks into the list.
- It's important to be able to point to the source for later discussions. Among other things, it proves that your research has been comprehensive.

Tasks	Overlap	Source
Book your GP appointment online	appointment	patients.co.uk
Let me book an appointment	appointment	user goals doc
Make an appointment	appointment	mayoclinic.com
Remind me when it's time for my appointment	appointment	user goals doc
Request an appointment	appointment	netwellness

We can see that the reason there is so much overlap in the appointments task is that it has come from a variety of sources (mayoclinic.com, netwellness, patients.co.uk, etc.).

In highly political organizations, you can't be too careful in keeping track of what goes into the longlist. Much later in the process, even when results are communicated, someone (usually someone important) may ask whether one or other source (from their department), or one or other task (their department's activity) was added to the longlist. Being able to prove that your research was thorough is therefore very important.

When you are merging duplicates into a single line, you have two options for how you name the "Source":

1. "Multiple": This signifies that this task came from multiple sources.
2. In highly political environments, consider adding all the sources into the "Source" column.

Tasks	Overlap	Source
Book / make an appointment		patients.co.uk, user goals, mayoclinic, netwellness

Notes

- The "Notes" column is for writing quick notes about the tasks.
- Once you feel a discussion is getting stuck or going around in circles, make a note and move on to the next task. Leave the hardest, most problematic discussions until as late in the shortlisting process as possible. As the shortlisting process progresses, things tend to become more clear and consensus will emerge more easily.

Shortlisting: getting to your final list

Typically, it takes about six weeks to get to a final shortlist. By the end of week three, you should have all sources collected because you need to let the list settle so that everyone can get a feel for it.

Every time you make a significant change to the task list, make a copy.

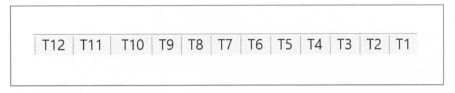

We use a very simple naming approach: "T1" for "Task list 1"; the very first list. Work from the left to the right, so the latest list you are working on will have the highest number. In Microsoft Excel, this will be positioned in first place at the bottom left of your spreadsheet.

There isn't usually a clean cut-off point from when you finish collecting all the possible tasks and start the shortlisting process. Usually, you can begin doing basic edits after collecting 30–40 percent of the tasks. But even once you get into serious shortlisting, you will still be adding some sources for a while.

Shortlisting works best when it is done in 90-minute to two-hour sessions. This is very intense work, so avoid doing this for more than two hours if possible. Aim to have no more than two to three shortlisting sessions per week.

For a large complex list, aim to have 6-8 sessions with the stakeholder group and another 6-8 administrative sessions tidying up the list and preparing for the next group session.

Shortlisting sessions

Administrative shortlisting

This is with your team (which might just be you!). The purpose of this is to clean up the list and get rid of items that can obviously be gotten rid of. Before every stakeholder shortlisting session, you should have an administrative one where you will:

- Implement actions as agreed in previous stakeholder sessions.
- Merge identically-worded tasks (exact duplicates).

- Tidy up layout and punctuation: Misspellings, misplaced commas, spacing, etc.
- Consolidate obvious overlaps.
- Categorize items into "Groups" and potentially "Sub-Groups". (This usually happens during the second or third session.)

Stakeholder shortlisting

These are the more formal sessions with the key stakeholders where all the major decisions should be made. Aim to start your first stakeholder shortlisting session with no more than 300 tasks. Again, the number of tasks is dependent on the complexity of the environment. In a typical situation, you will have around 200 tasks at the beginning of the first stakeholder shortlisting session. If the list is longer than 300, you might need to do some more administrative shortlisting to tidy things up more.

This is how a typical first stakeholder shortlisting session would look:

- Before the session starts, save a copy of the list in a new tab.
- Explain how the shortlisting works, how the columns in the spreadsheet are organized and the purpose of each column.
- Start with a quick read through the list to familiarize everyone with it. It is generally better if you or one of your colleagues read it aloud.
- Do not allow too much discussion on this first read through because otherwise, you won't get through it in the two hours you've allocated. Ask people to make notes about any issues they see coming up.
- At the end of the read-through, allow people to comment. If there is immediate consensus on certain things, make changes. Otherwise, add notes to the "Notes" column. Keep a quick pace.
- Look for universal consensus. Identify items that everyone immediately agrees should be deleted, merged, or further clarified. This is the best way to shortlist. If you hit major discussion areas, make a note in the "Notes" column and move on. Focus on what is easiest first. As the list gets smaller and stakeholders get more used to the process and the list itself, what might have required lots and lots of debate in an early session can often reach a rapid agreement as you near the end of the process.
- Do not worry about the "Group" or "Overlap" columns in the first session.

Wording for your tasks

Avoid verbs: It sounds counterintuitive, but even though grammatically a verb such as "find" or "get" might appear a good way of describing a task, such verbs can be confusing online. Use a noun to describe a task unless it's absolutely essential to use a verb in order to create clarity. For example, avoid writing "Get Pricing" — writing "Pricing" on its own is much better. (Or use "Prices".) The general rule is "lead with the need": cut to the essence, strip away everything that is not essential. If you start using verbs for every task, then you'll pollute your list with them, and it will become very hard to scan.

Use brackets where necessary: Brackets clarify the words before them. Only use brackets where you think the preceding task lacks clarity. The words in brackets do not need to be an exhaustive description of all the sub-tasks. Typically, two or three examples are sufficient. Do not use "etc." at the end of the bracket because otherwise your list will quickly fill with etcetera's and that will also make it harder to scan. Here's an example of using brackets in a local council/municipality task-list:

Conservation (ecology, nature, woodlands)

Length of task: Keep each task under 65 characters (8-10 words) if possible. The fewer words, the easier to scan.

Avoid repetition at the beginning of tasks: In your final list, ideally, every task on the list should begin with a unique word such as "pricing" or "installation". But this will not always be possible. You may have several tasks that need to begin with the name of the organization. Or if you are a product company you may need to have several tasks that begin with the word "product." Try and keep these to a minimum. In a list of 100 tasks, try and have no more than five that begin with the same word. Otherwise, the list will become more difficult to scan.

The list below is an example of how NOT to word tasks:

- European Commission at work
- European Commission competition
- European Commission directory
- European Commission economic forecasts
- European Commission education

- European Commission energy
- European Commission holidays
- European Commission human rights
- European Commission logo
- European Commission vacancies
- European Commission who is who
- European Commission youth

Deciding which tasks will stay and which will go

Duplicates, overlaps, mothers, and children

The first things you want to get rid of are exact duplicates, which will likely occur because you are gathering tasks from multiple sources. In one list, we found these exact duplicates:

- Check a VAT number
- Check a VAT number
- Check a VAT number

Just leave one and delete the rest. In the "Sources" column, it says something like "Multiple". This is the kind of housekeeping work you need to do in the administrative sessions. Avoid wasting time with stakeholders on minor issues like this.

That was the easy part! Overlaps are trickier. How would you deal with these items:

- Audit committee
- Audit policy
- Audit procedures
- Auditor certificate

The first step is to identify the core task and then use brackets for the subtasks. For example:

- Auditing (committees, policy, procedures, certificate)

Ultimately, you want to bring the brackets down to two to three items, but this is a start. Remember that "Auditing" might not even survive as a task. It might become part of "Accounting" or some higher-level task. But don't worry about that for now. Take one step at a time. Don't make big decisions in the early stages of shortlisting, just change things little by little.

Below is an example of what can be called a *mother* and *child:*

- anti-money laundering
- anti-corruption policy
- anti-corruption

"Anti-money laundering" is really a *child* of "anti-corruption". You want to avoid *mothers* and *children* appearing on the same list because this will create confusion, split the vote, and undermine the legitimacy of the results. For this example, consider doing the following:

- Anti-corruption (policy, anti-money laundering)

Remember, you're not trying to get everything perfect from the first session. You're just trying to clean the list up a bit and head in the right direction. Clear out what is obviously wrong. This is an iterative process, best done over two to three weeks. Hold a shortlisting session, and then leave it for a couple of days and come back to it. Then you should have a fresh perspective.

Here are another potential *mother* and *child*:

- Buy a book
- Most popular publications/bestsellers

"Most popular publications" is a *child* of "buying a book". Don't use brackets unless you think the task is unclear. "Buy a book" seems pretty clear on its own. Also, this is an example of where you would probably need a verb. If you just had "Books", the task would not be so obvious. But what about "publications" in "Most popular publications/bestsellers"? Does "publications" have a broader meaning than simply books in your organization? This is an ideal discussion point for your key stakeholders.

Here are another *mother* and *child:*

- Ask the Economists
- Find an expert

The *mother* is "Find an expert". You could reorganize it like this:

- Find an expert (economists)

Do you really need the brackets? Don't add them just for the sake of it. And, of course, if you do add the brackets, you will need more information than just "economists".

How would you deal with these tasks?

- Campus locations, opening hours
- Campus maps, directions, parking, contact info
- Parking

This may be a good solution:

- Campus directions, maps, parking, contact info, opening hours

Here we avoid brackets but rather let the sentence flow.

How would you restructure the following:

- Debt recovery and late payments
- Invoicing and payment management

It would seem that invoicing is a separate, though related, task to payment management. Perhaps they could be coupled later as one task, but at this stage, you may want to write them as:

- Payment management (debt recovery, late payments)
- Invoicing

What would you do with these items:

- Energy efficiency
- Reduce my energy/fuel-use and carbon emissions

This is a definite example of *mother* and *child*, with the *mother* being "Energy efficiency."

What about these tasks:

- Animal Protection
- Animal rights

This might be an appropriate solution:

- Animals (protection, rights)

What about these tasks for a university:

- Acceptance criteria

- Admission criteria, requirements

There is definite overlap here. What is the most common word? "Acceptance" or "admission"? For now, we can leave it as the following:

- Acceptance/admission criteria, requirements

How would you rearrange these tasks:

- Competition report
- Competition
- Competition policy and effects on business
- Competition rules

The following would work well:

- Competition (reports, policy, rules)

How would you deal with these tasks:

- Customer opportunities, pain points
- Customer satisfaction results
- How to discover how much budget your customer has?
- Market research

This example is not so simple. Clearly, "Market research" is a *mother* task. And "How to discover how much budget your customer has?" sounds quite micro and low-level. You might start like this:

- Market research (customer opportunities, pain points, satisfaction results, how much budget customer has)

Obviously, this title is far too long and cluttered. It consists of 13 words and over 100 characters. The maximum should be using is about 65 characters or eight words. But it's a start. Move on. You can come back later. A lot of this sort of work can be done in internal sessions with your own core team, but if you are doing that then be very careful about deletion. Just add to your brackets.

One other reason to add to the brackets and not to delete too soon is for later reference. When, for example, you are building the website after the top task identification and when you are preparing content briefs, you may need to go back to the early tables of the longlist to check out what exactly the elements were that went into that task line. You may need to "unpack" the task later, so to speak.

Also, you need to begin to use your "Overlap" column. If you're in any sort of doubt, avoid putting items together. Just add a common word in the "Overlap" column that allows the team to focus on this group of tasks. It's good to also have at least some of these overlap discussions in the shortlisting sessions with stakeholders because it makes them feel more involved in the process.

Here's an example of overlapping in action for Liverpool City Council:

Tasks	Overlap
Council housing	Housing
Home ownership	Housing
Homeless (family, single)	Housing
Housing	Housing
Housing allocations / eligibility advice	Housing
Housing benefit	Housing
Propertypool (choice based lettings)	Housing
Social housing	Housing
Supported and sheltered accommodation	Housing

How many distinct tasks are here? After our shortlisting discussions, we ended up with two tasks:

- Housing (council, social, associations, PropertyPool)
- Housing benefit

See how we dealt with the brand "PropertyPool", as brand names rarely clearly describe what the task is. As a rule, never have a brand name leading a task description. If the brand name is really popular, then put it in the brackets.

As you get near the end of the shortlisting process, you'll begin to address issues of balance and equivalence. In a list of 70 tasks, should there be two separate tasks for housing? Is housing that important? Does housing deserve to be in the final list at all? These crucial questions become a lot easier to answer after you have spent weeks with the list making it shorter and developing consensus with your stakeholders.

As the list gets shorter, and you've spent more time with it, things become clearer. You should be looking for balance. Remember, your final list should be under 100 tasks. (The minimum number of tasks for this sort of method to work is about 30.) Each task should be in balance with the other tasks on the list. They should all roughly be at the same level of importance and weight, all roughly equal. And they should be mutually exclusive.

What would you do with these tasks:

- Product interoperability
- Product quick overview
- Product technical information (part numbers, manuals, specifications, quick reference guide, installation)
- Product summaries
- Product photos, images
- Product features, benefits
- Product upgrades
- Pricing
- Release and tech notes
- Technical documentation (installation, administration, specifications, configuration, maintenance, operation)
- Technical information (requirements, white papers)

Figuring out a distinct set of clearly worded customer tasks can prove to be a headache. It requires a huge amount of mental effort, thought, and discussion. That's why most organizations avoid it. It's too hard because ultimately it's all about the simplification and organization of information which is hard work. It's much easier just to do a redesign with some nice graphics, to buy a new search engine or content management system. Migration is not nearly as difficult. Lots of manual labor, sure, but you will just be moving things from one place to another. There is less brainpower involved. My apologies, but for shortlisting, you will have to think—really think. What is it that you *are* as an organization? What's your *purpose*? What are your customers' tasks?

The way to deal with complexity is, little by little, to break it up into smaller, more manageable parts. There seem to be two broad groups of tasks in the list we just looked at. Firstly, we have general marketing-type information about the product:

- Product quick overview
- Product summaries
- Product photos, images
- Product features, benefits
- Pricing

Then we have more detailed technical information about the product:

- Product interoperability
- Product technical information (part numbers, manuals, specifications, quick reference guide, installation)
- Product upgrades
- Release and tech notes
- Technical documentation (installation, administration, specifications, configuration, maintenance, operation, troubleshooting)
- Technical information (requirements, white papers)

You need a lot of deep discussion with experts on the product, support, marketing, and sales to clarify and simplify these items. In the technical product tasks, we have two that are particularly problematic:

- Technical documentation (installation, administration, specifications, configuration, maintenance, operation, troubleshooting)
- Technical information (requirements, white papers)

Like the word "tools", the words "documentation" and "information" are problematic words from a task perspective. They are so broad they essentially become meaningless. They become the *mother* of all *mothers*. Let's look at this example:

- Technical documentation (installation, administration, specifications, configuration, maintenance, operation, troubleshooting)

In a technical product environment, this contains hugely important tasks such as:

- Installation, configuration

- Maintenance
- Using the product, operation
- Administration
- Troubleshooting

So, sometimes you will not be bringing together a group of tasks, but rather unpacking one that contains too many other important tasks.

In this example, how many distinct tasks can you identify:

- Business and deployment planning
- Business configurator
- Configuring a product for a quote, research
- Design planning, configuration, reference architecture
- Installation (configuration, setup, deployment)
- Product configuration
- Product deployment plan (country, product, number of machines)

It really depends on the organization and the type of business they're in. However, there are patterns that emerge wherever highly technical products are sold, because such products tend to be solutions—a combination or products, software, and services. Thus:

- Pre-purchase configuration for the purpose of getting a price/quote, and to ensure the configuration does meet your needs.
- Post-purchase configuration, which often goes hand in hand with installation. Deployment (which is the rollout of the installation) is also linked here but sometimes deployment can be a major task in its own right. It depends on the technical product in question.

What should be becoming very clear now is that you can't develop a good final task list without a thorough understanding of what the organization does and what the customer wants. You need the right stakeholders to be engaged in order to get to a quality shortlist.

How would you deal with the following tasks:

- Adoption and fostering
- Adult (abuse, protection, care)
- Child (cruelty, protection, abuse, care)
- Childcare

- Discrimination or harassment
- Domestic violence
- Elder abuse
- Family placement
- Nuisance/anti-social behavior
- Victim support

We've got two broad types of tasks here: "adult" and "child".

A. Adult
  - Adult (abuse, protection, care)
  - Discrimination or harassment
  - Domestic violence
  - Elder abuse
  - Nuisance/anti-social behavior
  - Victim support
B. Child
  - Childcare
  - Child cruelty, protection, abuse
  - Family placement

But what do you think of "Nuisance/anti-social behavior"? Is that really part of the first group, or should it be a task on its own? In many task-lists that we have developed with councils/municipalities, we ended up treating this as a task in its own right.

With one particular council, we ended up having these tasks for children:

- Adoption and fostering
- Child protection
- Childcare

We also included:

- Adult abuse (reporting, protecting)
- Community safety (crime and anti-social behavior)

How would you deal with the following:

- Accidents, emergencies, and safety
- Contact emergency services
- Emergency services

- Firefighting and rescue services
- Fire prevention

  It seems we have two types of tasks:

- Safety and accident prevention
- Emergency services, contact

  How would you arrange these tasks:

- Benefits
- Benefits 10-Day Promise
- Benefits and allowances
- Benefits new claim
- Benefits query
- Benefits reporting a change

  We could really simplify these to:

- Benefits and allowances (claims, queries, changes)

Do we even need the brackets? Probably not. The branding "Benefits 10-Day Promise" is equally unnecessary. Of course, the promise that you get a benefits decision in ten days or less is great, but it's not something to include in a task list. Avoid brands unless they have become synonymous with the task.

How could these tasks be simplified:

- Training agenda
- Training description, outline, overview, benefits

  Is the agenda part of the description? This is something to be discussed.

  How would you deal with this list of tasks? How much overlap is here?

- Assess your risk of a condition/disease
- Calculate your risk of a condition/disease
- How healthy am I? (Calculator)
- Health check to find out if you have a condition disease
- Self-assessment survey
- Self-assessment measure
- Diagnosis for a condition/disease
- Discover possible causes of your symptoms
- Do I have a condition/disease?

- Causes of a disease/condition
- Check your risk level
- Check your symptoms
- I have a condition. What are the symptoms of this condition?
- I have a symptom, is it normal?
- I have a symptom; what condition could it be?
- I have an embarrassing symptom. Where can I read about it without talking to my doctor?

There are some clearly distinct tasks here:

- Check symptoms
- Calculate risk of getting a condition/disease
- Health check/how healthy am I?
- Causes of a condition/disease

How would you simplify these tasks:

- Help me talk to my doctor/medical people about this condition
- I have a condition. How do I communicate with a health professional about an aspect of my treatment or condition?
- Prepare to talk with your Doctor
- Talking to your doctor
- Tips for talking to your doctor

There seems to be just one task here about getting help in order to have a useful chat with your doctor. The client we worked with ultimately chose the following:

- What to ask my doctor

Look at this list of potential tasks:

- I need a health service that is open late
- I need a local one that's open at an appropriate time
- I'd like to know if I/my child can see a GP if we are on holiday in the UK away from home
- It's late at night. Where can I get treatment now?
- Tell me which local GP/dentist has evening appointments

We chose:

- Opening times (GPs, clinics, chemists)

Where possible, avoid any sort of sentence construction beginning with "I'd like to" or "I need to". If you do that, then the tasks will be very hard to scan because a great many of them will be beginning the same way; they will be overly long, and they will contain unnecessary and redundant language. You must be ruthless when editing. Every word on the task-list should earn its place. Strip everything away that isn't absolutely necessary.

How about these tasks?

- Class experience (size, diversity, industry experience)
- Faculty-to-student ratio
- Flexible class schedules (online, on-campus, both)
- Program delivery (online, on-campus)

Actually, this was a bit of a trick question. The client felt that all the above tasks were distinct, and they decided to keep them all.

What about these tasks? This is an obvious example of a *mother* and *children* at play:

- Accessories and parts
- Parts inventory management system
- Parts recommendation tool
- Parts issue handling system
- Parts sales administration
- Parts supply chain
- Parts templates (repurchase, return, etc.)
- Pricing of parts
- Spare part kits
- Spare part support (operating hours, 24-hour emergency service)
- Spare parts

How many "spare parts"-related tasks should you have on the list? Again, it depends on the nature of the business. For a business selling simpler products, then "Accessories and parts" may be fine. But for a business where spare parts are a big element of the revenue, then something more may be needed. Certainly, in such a business, you would not combine "accessories" and "parts" in the same phrase.

What about these two?

- Contact support
- Support requests (open, check status, escalate)

Have you ever run up against a conflict between a customer need and an organization need? The customer just wants to contact support and get their problem solved as quickly as possible. The organization wants them to open a more formal support request, so that they can more efficiently and cost-effectively track and manage the process. The option which ultimately gets chosen depends on the nature of the organization and the traditional nature of the relationship between the organization and its customers.

These are tasks from an intranet:

- Compliance (safety, health, environmental, import-export)
- Corporate governance
- Global processes
- Information security
- Operational guidelines
- Processes, procedures, policies, guidelines, standards
- Working remotely
- World Class Manufacturing (WCM)

Clearly, the following tasks directly overlap:

- Global processes
- Operational guidelines
- Processes, procedures, policies, guidelines, standards

"Global processes" and "Operational guidelines" are *children* of the *mother* task, "Processes, procedures…." Strictly speaking, "Processes, procedures, policies, guidelines, standards" and "Information security" are apples and oranges. Really, the process or procedure should come under the appropriate task. So, under "Information security" there should be a range of tasks including information security processes and procedures. Under "Corporate governance", we should find the relevant processes and procedures. That's not how many organizations are designed today, though. They are designed in silos. There is a document management system where all—or at least a significant quantity—of the processes and procedures are held.

So, what do you do in the task-list? We have been doing task identification for more than 15 years. In the early years, we left tasks such as "Processes,

Procedures …" in the list because we came across them so often that we wanted to gauge just how important they were. However, in recent years, we have discussed these issues and come to an agreement that procedures and policies are a given in any intranet/digital workplace. They're going to be there and we're going to place them with their relevant tasks.

So, for example, in the BBC intranet, if you want to book a taxi or courier, you go to the page for "Booking a taxi" and there you clearly see a link to the policy and procedure for booking taxis. When you run shortlisting sessions with a diverse range of stakeholders you tend to have these sorts of important discussions. The shortlist of tasks under negotiation are the essential building blocks for your future digital world. It'll end up being a small final list (typically between 50 and 80), but its potential impact is very significant.

What about these tasks:

- Product lifecycle needs
- Product lifecycle
- Product phase out
- End of sale/end of life

Here there are two tasks, really:

- Product lifecycle
- End of sale, end of life, product phase out

What would you do with these tasks:

- Search by age and gender
- Search by A-Z
- Search by name or health topic
- Search by parts of the body
- Search by subject index
- Search by symptom
- Search for doctors, dentists, pharmacies (chemists), hospitals, walk-in centers and many more services
- Symptom Search

Generally, we don't use the word "search" at all in our task lists. "Search" is a given, just as "navigate" is. Here, we might use tasks such as:

- Check symptoms

- Find a doctor

Avoid departments, brands, products, subject areas

You will need to remove brands, product names, department names, and subject areas from the list:

- In a university task-list, do not have the names of the courses (English, Computer Science, Law, etc.).
- In an intranet task-list, do not have a list of the departments (HR, IT, Accounting).
- In a company task-list, do not have a list of the products.
- In a healthcare task-list, do not have a list of the diseases/conditions.

You want tasks that are universal—that work across brands, products, diseases, and departments. No matter what the product, "pricing" works as a task. No matter what the disease, "check symptoms" works as a task.

In general, remove anything that sounds like branding. Have a look at these tasks:

- Investors in People
- Leadership/management development
- Training and developing staff

What does "Investors in People" mean to the average person? And how does it overlap with leadership development and staff training? Keep asking the really obvious questions. This is another reason why it's very important to have a broad range of people involved in shortlisting. The Human Resources people will assume everyone knows what "Investors in People" means, but time and time again we have found that departmental jargon can confuse and annoy. Your task-list simply won't work unless it's written in simple, clear language so that everyone you're asking to vote on it can instantly understand it.

You're just working with a handful of words, but these words can say a lot about the culture of the organization. Based on what follows, is the organization flat or hierarchical?

- Leadership/management development
- Training and developing staff

You might be wondering: "So, staff don't get leadership development? Only managers?" These are the type of discussions that should happen in shortlisting sessions. You have to try to get to the essence of what the organization is in the eyes of its customers or employees. The deeper the conversations, the more likely that the results can help facilitate real change towards a customer-centric, employee-centric culture.

What does "Observer Magazine" or "At A Glance" or "Marketing Central" mean, particularly to a potential customer? Does the "Observer Magazine" contain a whole group of tasks? Do people really want a magazine or a newspaper? Or do they want a whitepaper? Or just plain paper? What is a "whitepaper"? How is it different from green paper or blue paper? Don't be afraid to look stupid by asking very basic questions, because when you ask the most basic questions about wording, you often find out that people don't know why something was named the way it is: "It's just always been called that."

How about "IntelliTrace"? Sure, you knew that IntelliTrace helps you to debug code, didn't you? Why not just use "Debugging (diagnose, reproduce, fix)" then everyone immediately understands the task? And if the brand name is so popular that it has become synonymous with the task, then do this "Debugging (diagnose, reproduce, fix, IntelliTrace).

What does "Frank", "Avert", "Like It Is", and "Papyrus" mean to you? They're all meaningless, healthcare-related brands in the UK connected with teenage pregnancy, drug addiction, etc. Get behind the brand. Get to the essence of what the person wants to do.

Avoid Dirty Magnets and broad, meaningless terms

What do "Knowledge Base", or "Local Resources", or "Documents" mean? These are vague, meaningless terms or what I call *dirty magnets*. A *dirty magnet* is so vague, and yet appealing, that it can potentially mean anything to anyone. Thus, it can get a big vote, but for all sorts of reasons. What is in this "Knowledge Base"? What sort of "local resources" are we talking about? Get to the essence of the tasks and avoid those vague dirty magnets.

A classic dirty magnet is Frequently Asked Questions (FAQs): a terrible, lazy, organization-centric form of navigation. Think about it. A customer comes to your website with a task. How do they know that their particular task is a frequently asked question or not? If pricing, for example, is a frequently asked question, put that in the task-list. You must hunt down and remove all the jargon, the organization-think, and those vague, meaningless terms.

What does "Partner" mean? If you're a large, technology company then a partner is someone you sell your products through or collaborate with. However, if you're a customer are you looking for a "partner"? (If so, shouldn't you be on a dating website?) Or, perhaps you're looking for a reseller, a consultancy, or a shop? This may seem like trivial stuff, but it is actually central to a great customer experience. We worked with one client where we literally doubled sales inquiries by changing "Partner" to "Shop". Getting the words right in the tasks—there's nothing more important.

Avoid goals on your list. Here are some goals related to healthcare:

- I'd like to be happier
- I'd like to have more energy
- I'd like to improve my family's health
- I'd like to sleep better

These are great goals for people to have and most of us say these sort of things at various stages of our lives. But they're not good material for a task-list. When we go to the Web we have a task in mind connected with our goal. You'll say that you want to have more energy but when you search you're likely to use words like "diet" or "fitness". When you look at something on your list, ask this question: If it gets a big vote, what do we do? What sort of content and services do we create?

No audiences, demographics

Tasks should be universal. Remove the following types of tasks:

- Women's health
- Men's health

Instead, have:

- Check symptoms
- Treatment

It doesn't matter what your gender is, what your income is, or where you live, checking symptoms and getting treatment can still be relevant to you.

You don't want:

- Development policy for Austria
- Development policy for Ireland

Instead, have "Development policy." Then, if you decide, you can have a category/demographic question that asks people what country they come from.

Don't have:

- Training for developers
- Training for testers

Instead, have "Training" and then you can have a category question asking people if they are developers, testers, etc. Make your tasks as universal as possible.

Avoid formats, channels

Avoid formats such as "reports," "newsletters," "documents," "tools," "videos," "forms," and "templates." Avoid channels such as Twitter, Facebook, and YouTube. Always try and get to the tasks that these formats and channels support. There will always be exceptions. When we worked on the US Internal Revenue Service intranet, forms were central to our work because they use so many of them. But, in general, people are not looking for a form: they want to claim expenses, renew a driving license, return a product. Get to the tasks that the forms support.

There is a huge print legacy in the way we still name and organize things in our digital environments. People don't want documents or reports. They do want to install, troubleshoot, to get investment advice, to understand if one product works with another. Work to get behind whatever print legacy you have and bring out the true customer tasks.

Not too high, not too low

When you've finished the shortlisting process, all the tasks should be roughly at the same level of importance. If you imagine navigation on a typical website, then the top level is probably too high and level three is probably too low. Level two—the sections you get to when you click on a top-level navigation on the homepage is probably about right. Getting the level right will become easier as you get closer to the end of the shortlisting process, as you will have had lots of discussions and will be dealing with a much smaller list of tasks.

Let's look at a healthcare example. The following are too high-level:

- Facts and figures
- Conditions
- Diseases

- Find services
- Frequently asked health questions
- Injury prevention
- Medical conditions
- Mind, Body, & Spirit

    Whereas, the following are too low-level:

- Emergency contraception
- Nonprofit agencies
- Poems and stories about aging
- Cancer
- Diabetes
- Walk-in centers
- Animal companions
- Dealing with stress

As we can see, just having "diseases" is too high-level but listing all the diseases and conditions is too low-level. We need some sort of middle ground. Something like this:

- Diagnosis of condition/disease
- Living/coping with my condition/disease (support, counseling)
- Detailed information about condition/disease
- Self-management of a condition/disease
- Prognosis/likely course of condition/disease
- Treatment outcome (immediate, long-term)
- Seriousness of condition/disease
- Causes of condition/disease

Ego tasks

Consider allowing up to five percent of your task-list for *ego tasks*. These are tasks that the organization, and in particular senior management, feels very passionate about. They may include such tasks as:

- Senior management speeches
- Annual report
- Follow us on Twitter
- Videos

It's pretty certain that such ego tasks won't get much of a vote, but it can be important to include them on the final task-list just to show how unimportant they are to the customer.

Length of final shortlist

- A maximum of 100 tasks is recommended (though we have had lists that worked with up to 150 tasks).
- A minimum of 30 tasks is recommended.
- 50-80 is the typical length of a final task-list.

Designing the survey

Designing a Top Tasks question

What you are about to see is simply not common sense; it is counter-intuitive. But it has worked for more than 15 years in 30 languages with more than 300,000 people completing it successfully. We have not had one instance where we had to scrap the survey because people refused to do it, or we were getting poor quality results, but it does look weird, as you can see from what follows:

Select up to 5 tasks / resources (from the list below) that are MOST IMPORTANT to you when choosing a university.

**IMPORTANT: Select no more than five (5) from the list below.
LEAVE ALL THE REST BLANK.**

Please trust your first instincts and spend no more than 5 minutes on this exercise.

- How to choose a program
- Employment, placement, career success rate
- Admission (application deadline, decision date, application status)
- Profiles of faculty / professors
- Academic advisors to help to select classes
- Giving to the university (money, time expertise)
- Academic calendar
- Registration for classes
- Update my address
- Cost of living (housing / accommodation, food, transport)
- Value of your degree / education / return on Investment
- Alumni profiles
- News
- Manage classes / courses (add, drop, change)
- Transfer agreements with two-year colleges
- Course ranking and ratings
- Class schedules (online, on-campus, both
- Change degrees / program

What you have just seen is just a small sample, showing 18 tasks of what could be a 100-task survey question. When designing such a question:

- Put the **ENTIRE** final shortlist in one list in **ONE** column. (Yes, the final shortlist can be up to 100 tasks.) It is essential that you do not break up the list, otherwise, we cannot get a single league table of tasks.
- Put it into one, single scrolling page. Do not break it up into multiple columns or multiple sections.
- Randomize the list.

Framing the task question

Frame the question from the point of view of the person who will be voting, not from the point of view of the organization. Do not say:

"When using our website what are the five most important things to you?"

Instead, say:

"When dealing with health, choose up to five of the things most important to you."

Over the years, we have tested various ways to get people to choose. We tried asking people to choose ten tasks but found that was too difficult. We found that choosing five worked for most people.

Once people had selected their top five tasks, we used to ask them to rank those tasks, giving a "five" to the most important, a "four" to the next most important, and so on. When we analyzed a range of results, we noticed that statistically there was very little difference in the ranking results based on the vote a task had received and the number of people who voted for it. So, we simplified things: Now, we only ask people to choose tasks; they don't have to rank them.

Then, we tested again to try and simplify things yet further. We ran two identical surveys, one where people were asked to choose five, and the other where people could choose **up to** five. We found no statistical difference between the two sets of results. So, our instruction is: "Choose up to five…"

Here are some other examples of how you could introduce the task question:

- Please look at the following list and choose up to FIVE of the most important things for you when deciding to buy a new car.

- Below is a list of typical IT-related challenges that organizations face. Choose up to FIVE of the challenges you face with which you would consider seeking support from an external company.
- Select up to FIVE words or phrases from the following list that reflect the most important things to you in relation to a satellite navigation system.
- When interacting with the European Commission, choose up to five of the most important things for you.
- In managing a network, choose up to five of the most important things for you.

Why does this crazy approach work?

So, how do we know this crazy approach work, as it seems to break all the rules?

1. We have evidence it works. Since 2003, over 300,000 people have taken part in Top Tasks surveys in more than 30 languages and countries — students, teachers, doctors, nurses, consumers, engineers, old and young, employed and unemployed.
2. The sheer size of the list forces the gut instinct of the customer to kick in. We force them to select the things they really need, rather than the things they might like.
3. The tasks—and the wording of these tasks—comes mainly from the customers themselves. It is written in their language, in their words. The list reflects their world and what they think and care about.
4. The question is framed from the customers' perspective. It is written in a way which says, "help us make our website better!" but rather, "what's most important to you?" It's personal.

Category/demographic questions

You may want to know:

- If current customers have different tasks from potential customers.
- If there are differences in tasks depending on the customer's country of origin.
- If different professional roles have different tasks.
- If men and women have different top tasks, etc.

That's the purpose of category/demographic questions. Hence:

- Aim for about five, and no more than eight of such questions, as otherwise, the survey will become too long.
- Think carefully when selecting questions. Don't just add a question for the sake of it. Evaluate where you really need to differentiate between tasks of one group of people versus another.
- Consider your stakeholders very carefully when developing these questions. 'Our group of customers is different' is a classic initial response within organizations. The category questions will show whether, in fact, there are different tasks between groups, so it's very important you choose the questions carefully. This is a political issue.
- Aim for no more than eight sub-categories where possible within a particular category. (An example of a sub-category would be 'current customer' or 'potential customer.') To get reliable data on a particular sub-category you will need 25 or more people selecting that sub-category. Ideally, you should aim for 50 or more.
- Avoid making these questions mandatory. The more questions you force people to answer, the more likely it is they will abandon the questionnaire.

	Tasks	England	Scotland	Wales	Northern Ireland	Total
1	Cashflow, invoicing, payment management	6.0%	6.8%	6.6%	6.3%	6.3%
2	Marketing	4.9%	4.9%	6.4%	6.1%	5.6%
3	Productivity / profitability	4.0%	8.4%	5.5%	5.5%	5.0%
4	Funding / finance sources	3.0%	2.6%	4.5%	4.4%	3.6%
5	Managing people	2.7%	5.9%	3.4%	4.3%	3.4%
6	Accounting, financial management	3.2%	3.7%	3.3%	3.1%	3.3%
7	Grants, benefits, entitlements from government	2.6%	2.6%	4.2%	3.1%	3.2%
8	Selling (legal, e-commerce, pricing)	3.2%	3.4%	2.8%	3.4%	3.1%
9	Create business plan, budget	2.9%	2.4%	2.5%	2.9%	2.7%
10	Website design, management, optimisation	2.6%	1.7%	2.8%	3.0%	2.7%
11	Health and safety at work	2.1%	2.5%	3.5%	1.8%	2.5%
12	New ideas (products, services, green)	1.8%	3.7%	2.8%	2.3%	2.3%
13	Public sector contracts, tenders	1.5%	1.5%	3.6%	1.7%	2.2%
14	Training and development	1.7%	1.8%	2.8%	2.5%	2.2%
15	Tax returns (complete, amend)	2.7%	1.2%	1.6%	1.9%	2.1%
16	Suppliers, outsourcing, partnering	1.6%	1.5%	1.5%	1.7%	1.6%
17	Debt recovery, late payments	1.3%	2.6%	1.4%	2.4%	1.6%
18	Standards (quality, safety, environment)	1.6%	2.3%	1.3%	1.7%	1.6%
19	Paying, payroll, taxing staff	1.9%	0.9%	1.3%	1.8%	1.6%
20	Form a company, business	1.9%	0.7%	0.8%	1.3%	1.4%

- This was a Top Tasks survey of UK businesses carried out in 2010.

- The table is sorted based on the 'Total' column.
- Businesses were asked about where they were based.
- Top Tasks—those that reached the top 50 percent of the vote—are shaded in grey.
- Tiny tasks—those that were in the bottom 50 percent of the vote—are in white.
- We can quickly see that the top tasks are essentially the same, regardless of what country a business is based in.

Practically every time we start Top Tasks, the organization will say: "Our organization is very complicated. It is unique. And our customers are particularly unique. We predict huge differences in tasks between customer categories." And when the results roll in we nearly always find far more similarities in top tasks across customer categories than was expected. However, there can, of course, be some interesting differences, as we can see from the following table. Here, the category question asked whether people were self-employed, employed, or starting a business.

	Tasks	Self employed / Business owner	Employed	Starting a business	Total
1	Cashflow, invoicing, payment management	7.3%	6.0%	4.4%	6.3%
2	Marketing	6.2%	3.8%	6.0%	5.6%
3	Productivity / profitability	5.6%	5.9%	3.2%	5.0%
4	Funding / finance sources	3.2%	3.7%	4.4%	3.6%
5	Managing people	3.6%	5.9%	0.9%	3.4%
6	Accounting, financial management	3.4%	3.9%	2.3%	3.3%
7	Grants, benefits, entitlements from government	2.8%	2.4%	5.5%	3.2%
8	Selling (legal, e-commerce, pricing)	3.7%	2.6%	3.1%	3.1%
9	Create business plan, budget	1.9%	2.4%	4.8%	2.7%
10	Website design, management, optimisation	3.1%	1.3%	3.6%	2.7%
11	Health and safety at work	2.5%	4.0%	1.5%	2.5%
12	New ideas (products, services, green)	3.0%	2.2%	0.9%	2.3%
13	Public sector contracts, tenders	2.5%	2.6%	1.1%	2.2%
14	Training and development	2.4%	2.1%	1.6%	2.2%
15	Tax returns (complete, amend)	2.3%	1.2%	1.8%	2.1%
16	Suppliers, outsourcing, partnering	1.6%	1.6%	1.7%	1.6%
17	Debt recovery, late payments	2.2%	1.4%	0.3%	1.6%
18	Standards (quality, safety, environment)	1.6%	1.9%	1.3%	1.6%
19	Paying, payroll, taxing staff	1.1%	2.6%	1.2%	1.6%
20	Form a company, business	0.4%	0.7%	5.2%	1.4%

- Overall, top tasks are very similar.
- However, we notice that for those starting a business, "managing people" is a tiny task. This might be because when starting a business, often you

will only have a few employees. Or perhaps, those starting a business underestimate the true challenges of managing people?

- A top task for those starting a business is "form a company/business." It is their third most important task. Whereas, for those already in business, it is a tiny task. This, of course, makes sense.

But what the preceding two tables tell us is that we should avoid separate classifications for each country. We also do not need classifications for clients who are self-employed, employed, and starting a business. (At least, not at the top level.) Instead, we can have classifications called: 'Cash flow', 'Marketing', 'Productivity', 'Funding', 'Managing people', etc.

In a typical Top Tasks survey, the first category question and usually the first question in the survey will go something like this:

What is your relationship with:

- Employees
- Potential customers
- Current customers seeking support
- Current customers evaluating a purchase
- Partners
- Media/journalists/analysts
- Students
- Job seekers
- Other

Here's the first question for a council/municipality:

I am visiting (select all that apply):

- as a parent
- as a student
- as a carer
- as a retired person
- as a business owner
- as a visitor to the area
- as a council employee
- in some other capacity

For a university, the introductory question might be:

What best describes your current situation relative to this university?

- Considering or applying to …
- A student at …
- A member of faculty or staff
- An ex-student (alumni)

The reason we have this type of question is to allow the organization to filter out certain sub-categories, if they so choose. For example, you might not want students and job seekers to take a particular survey, so if someone selects either of these sub-categories, then they are routed out of the survey and sent to a 'Thank you' page.

Immediately after this type of question, we tend to find the core question asking people to choose up to five of their top tasks from the final shortlist of tasks. We usually then ask the following questions:

How often do you use the website/app?

- Daily
- Weekly
- Monthly
- Infrequently
- First time

For those who answer "daily", "weekly", or "monthly" to the above question, we would ask this question:

Are you usually able to find what you are looking for or complete your task on the website/app?

- Yes
- No

This is a very useful question: if your "no" answers are above 20% then you are in big trouble with your customers.

Next, we tend to have the Customer Centric Index, which is designed to find out what element of the website/app customers most want to see improved. It is presented in the same way as the Top Tasks question.

Select up to three factors from the list below that best describe your experience when trying to complete tasks on the...

Important: Select no more than three from the list below. Leave the rest blank.

- Accurate information
- Clear menus and links
- Cluttered layout / hard to read
- Complete information
- Confusing menus and links
- Easy to contact a person
- Easy to participate / give feedback
- Fast to do things
- Fast to do things

(You can run the Customer Centric Index independently of a Top Tasks survey. Find out more here: www.customercentricindex.com)

Here is a list of other category/demographic questions that you might want to ask:

- What is the size of the organization that the person works for?
- In which country or region do they live?
- What product category/type of product interests them?
- What is their professional role?
- What is their gender?
- What age are they?
- What is their income?
- Are they visiting the website for themselves or someone else?
- What type of industry or sector do they work in?
- Would they like to make any comments?
- Would they like to help in the future by giving feedback on the website/app? This would require them to give their name and email address. We've found this question particularly useful.

For intranets, typical questions include the following:

Who do you collaborate with?

- Colleagues in my department
- Other departments
- External stakeholders

How often do you collaborate with colleagues outside your department?

- Every day
- Every week
- Every month
- Less often
- Never

What are the main barriers for you in collaborating with colleagues outside your department?

- Difficult to find the right person or community to collaborate with
- Lack of training in collaborative tools and techniques
- No culture or tradition of collaboration
- No encouragement or reward for collaboration
- Other departments are seen as competitors
- People keep their expertise and information to themselves
- Poor quality tools available for collaboration
- Time-consuming. This type of collaboration slows down work delivery

Do you manage people?

- Yes
- No

What is your professional role?

- IT
- Support
- HR
- Marketing
- Sales
- Technical, etc.

Team/stakeholder survey

Once you've finalized your survey, create a copy of it and ask your internal team/stakeholders to participate in a vote.

- Reword the introduction to the Top Tasks question to something like: "What do you think your customers' most important tasks are? Select up to five."
- Most of the category questions will not be suitable, so delete them. You might need to add a few specific category questions to understand who is voting from your stakeholders.
- You will need at least 15 stakeholders voting in order to get useful results.

Encouraging people to vote

Top Tasks surveys are conducted using an online survey tool such as 'SurveyMonkey'. The best way to get people to take the survey is by using a popup window. 'Popups' are certainly annoying, but they still work much better than simply having a banner or other communication on a page. Another option is to use an email invitation sent to a targeted subscriber list.

Incentives and prizes will improve participation. However, depending on the target audience, you receive a lower quality of response, as some will complete the survey purely for the incentive. Incentives can be quite time-consuming to set up, and there are often legal implications, such as collection of personal information, offering prizes, etc. So, if you are considering incentives, you need to plan well in advance.

When creating the invitation text to take the survey, do not make the common mistake of asking people to take a survey. "Take our survey" or "Help us improve our website" is a very organization-centric message and unlikely to yield a good response. Frame the message from the point of view of the customer. Here are some examples:

What are your tasks when you are managing a network? Tell us so we can make things better for you.

What's most important to you when dealing with your health? Let us know so that we can better serve you.

When buying a car, what matters most to you?

Number of voters required

400 people are required to vote on the task-list to deliver reliable data. However, you can get also good results with about 200 people, and even 100 people will give you a strong indication of what the top three tasks are. In fact, for the European Commission survey, which included 107,000 participants, the top three tasks had emerged after surveying just 30 participants. Yes, after 30 participants the top three tasks were exactly the same as after 107,000.

For a sub-category, you need at least about 50 people. Certainly, you should aim for a minimum of 25, though I have seen useful data emerge from as few as 15 participants. The number of people you need for a sub-category is relative to the overall poll size. If you have 200 people responding, then 25 in one particular sub-category can be sufficient, but if you have 2,000 people responding, you should really have at least 50 in a sub-category before you allow it to be analyzed. Take the example below:

	Percent	Response
Africa	5%	98
Asia & Pacific	16%	339
Europe	55%	1158
Middle East	1%	18
North America	20%	424
South America	4%	83
	Total	2120

It would not be appropriate to analyze the data from the Middle East, for example, from the above table, because response rates are significantly lower than all the other sub-categories. Monitor the sub-categories as the survey progresses, and if an important sub-category has a low number of participants, then take action to increase representation in that category.

Analyzing and presenting results

Create a presentation with the following sequence:

Survey period, number of participants

- Over what period was this survey conducted? (For example: From July 1st to August 1st)
- Number of participants

Customer category segmentation

Information on who voted broken down by category questions. Each category question should have a table something like the following:

How often do you use our website?

	Percent	Response
Daily	16%	84
Weekly	33%	177
Monthly	12%	65
Infrequently	19%	101
First time	19%	103
	Total	530

It's important to analyze who responded at the very beginning so that your audience is comfortable that survey participants are representative of the target group.

The final list of tasks used in a survey

Present the list of the tasks used in the survey. At this point in the presentation, you may explain the sources of these tasks and the collaborative process that led to the final, agreed list.

Vote trend analysis

Here you seek to build confidence in the results by showing that they are statistically reliable. We use the following table to show how results have stabilized. For the purposes of simplicity, we have marked the top tasks (top 50 percent of the vote) in light grey, and the tiny tasks (the remaining 50 percent of the vote) in white.

	Tasks	¼ of voters	½ of voters	¾ of voters	100% of voters
1	Business opportunities (call for tenders, bids)	6.0%	6.3%	6.5%	6.5%
2	Scholarship program	5.3%	5.2%	5.7%	5.4%
3	Economic research, forecasting, analysis	5.3%	5.4%	5.1%	5.2%
4	Download, browse publications	3.9%	4.3%	4.3%	4.5%
5	Project implementation lessons learned, good practices	5.0%	4.3%	4.5%	4.4%
6	Country statistical data, indicators	4.8%	4.4%	3.9%	4.1%
7	Project pipeline, proposed projects	3.2%	4.0%	4.0%	3.9%
8	Training, e-learning	3.9%	4.0%	4.2%	3.8%
9	Country strategy, plans	3.6%	3.2%	3.4%	3.2%
10	Collaborate, share knowledge, network with peers, ADB experts	2.7%	2.7%	2.8%	3.0%
11	Development achievements, effectiveness (roads built, children in school, gender inclusiveness)	2.7%	3.3%	3.2%	3.0%
12	Access raw data, datasets from projects	3.1%	2.9%	3.2%	2.9%
13	Development news and articles	3.0%	3.2%	2.8%	2.7%
14	Case studies	3.4%	3.2%	2.9%	2.6%
15	News (loans, reports, events, management activities)	2.5%	2.6%	2.2%	2.5%
16	Events, workshops	2.9%	2.4%	2.1%	2.3%
17	Project monitoring, performance, status updates	2.1%	1.8%	2.1%	2.3%
18	Public-private partnerships	1.9%	2.3%	2.2%	2.2%
19	Organization strategy	2.5%	2.3%	2.0%	2.2%
20	Approved projects	2.7%	2.4%	2.4%	2.2%

- There were 600 voters in this survey.
- We show how the vote looked after 150 voters (first quarter of voters), 300 voters, 450 voters, and at the end of the survey when 600 voters had voted.
- See how the grey is solidly consistent from the first quarter onwards. We can see that the top tasks emerged very quickly, as they nearly always do. We could probably have stopped the survey at 150 voters and we would already have the top tasks.
- Showing this table to stakeholders gives them confidence that the data is solid and reliable.

The following chart is a different approach to looking at voting trends:

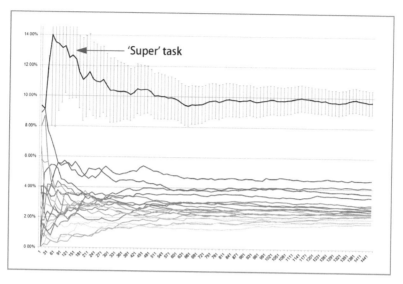

- From this particular chart, we can clearly see that a 'super' task has emerged and has left all the other tasks way behind.
- It was first from the first voter and raced way ahead of everything else.
- According to the statistical analysis we do, the chances of this particular task being second are infinitesimal - there's no chance.
- The grey lines indicate the possible variance for this task. At the end of the survey, it had about 9.8% of the vote. According to the grey bands, it could have gone as high as 10.5% of the vote, or as low as 9% of the vote. (We use 95% confidence intervals.)
- Booking a flight on an airline site or booking a room on a hotel website are examples of supertasks. When you encounter a supertask, it needs to be made immediately accessible from the very first screen.

Overall results

Present the results in four distinct quartiles:

1. First 25%: These are the most important top tasks.
2. 25% to 50%: These are also top tasks. Basically, the first 50% of the vote is your top tasks list.
3. 50% to 75%: These are less important tasks.
4. 75% to 100%: These are the true tiny tasks.

The following chart shows how the results generally look when there are 100 tasks in the final task-list:

- The top five tasks get the first 25% of the vote.
- 10 tasks get the next 25% of the vote.
- 35 tasks get the next 25%.
- 50 tasks get the final 25%.
- So, the top five tasks get as much of the vote as the bottom 50.

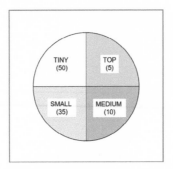

This basic pattern repeats itself year-in, year-out, across 30 different languages, in over 30 countries, with hundreds of thousands of engineers, doctors, citizens, football fans, researchers, men and women, old and young, rich and poor, whether people are buying cars or dealing with a disease. The pattern just keeps repeating itself.

Shouldn't we be focusing on the top five? Instead, what we find is that the organization is often focusing time and energy on the bottom 50 because these tiny tasks are highly political and 'ambitious' (Remember how when a tiny task goes to sleep at night it dreams of being a top task?).

As this section of the book was being written, a Top Tasks survey was being completed. Here's what it looked like:

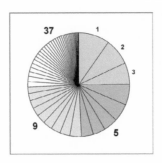

- There were 54 tasks in the final shortlist.
- 3 got as much of the vote as the bottom 37.
- In fact, the top task got as much of the vote as the bottom 23.
- This sort of data gives you the whole justification for focusing on top tasks.

We get more detailed analysis of the voting in the following table. This example is from the Organization for Economic Co-operation and Development (OECD). Below is a description of the various categories.

	Tasks	Total Vote	% of Total Vote 31800	Cumulative Vote	Cumulative Tasks
1	Country surveys / reviews / reports	2178	6.8%	6.8%	1.4%
2	Compare country statistical data	1960	6.2%	13.0%	2.9%
3	Statistics on one particular topic	1869	5.9%	18.9%	4.3%
4	Browse a publication online for free	1610	5.1%	24.0%	5.7%
5	Working papers	1530	4.8%	28.8%	7.1%
6	Publication by topic	1478	4.6%	33.4%	8.6%
7	Basic facts, summaries and overviews	1379	4.3%	37.7%	10.0%
8	Statistics on one particular country	1285	4.0%	41.8%	11.4%
9	Statistical forecasts / projections	1210	3.8%	45.6%	12.9%
10	Access to raw data	1051	3.3%	48.9%	14.3%
11	International guidelines and standards (corporate governance, tax havens, etc.)	1025	3.2%	52.1%	15.7%
12	Statistical sources and methods	1019	3.2%	55.3%	17.1%
13	What's new (hot topics, recent publications, events)	1004	3.2%	58.5%	18.6%
14	OECD policy advice by topic, country	843	2.7%	61.1%	20.0%
15	OECD Annual Report	784	2.5%	63.6%	21.4%
16	Publication by country	746	2.3%	65.9%	22.9%
17	Best practice in policy implementation	739	2.3%	68.3%	24.3%
18	Publication by title	614	1.9%	70.2%	25.7%
19	Simple, easy-to-understand tables and graphs	613	1.9%	72.1%	27.1%
20	News releases	542	1.7%	73.8%	28.6%

- **Total Vote:** The votes cast for a particular task. The top task — "Country surveys/reviews/reports" — received 2,178 votes.
- **% of Total Vote:** The 2,178 votes for "Country surveys" represents 6.8% of the total votes cast of 31,800 votes.
- **Cumulative Vote:** This indicates how much of the total vote has been given to a certain number of tasks. So, we can see that the cumulative vote for the first three tasks is 18.9%.
- **Cumulative tasks:** In this particular poll, there were 70 tasks in the final list. As a percentage, this means that one task represents 1.43%. Thus, two tasks round up to 2.9%. Remember our 5:25 rule — that 5% of the tasks will win 25% of the vote? Well, in this particular survey, we instead see 5.7% of the tasks winning 24% of the vote, which is pretty close.

Over the years, we have changed the voting approach. It used to be that you had to select your top five and then give a rating out of five according to their importance for you, with a 'five' for the most important, a 'four' for the next most important, and so on. But when we compared the number of voters for a task versus the number of votes it received, we found essentially the same ranking order. So, for the purposes of simplicity, we now only ask people to choose up to five.

The next chart that we use shows the long neck/long tail concept:

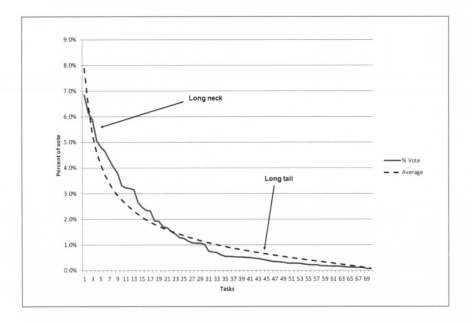

- **Long neck:** the small set of tasks at the left of the graph have won a large proportion of the vote.
- **Long tail:** A large number of tiny tasks that, individually, each received a very small proportion of the vote.
- **Dotted line:** This is the average pattern that has been found over the 400-plus Top Tasks surveys that we have conducted.
- **Full line:** These were the voting results for this particular survey. We can see that both curves match pretty well, although the actual line here is a bit 'fatter' than average. The top task, with almost 7% of the vote, is lower

than average with just under 8%. (These average percentages are relative to the number of tasks in a particular survey.)

We also use the following table to show what the long tail looks like:

Tasks	Total Vote	% of Total Vote 31800	Cumulative Vote	Cumulative Tasks
51 Find a local library with OECD publications	92	0.3%	96.7%	72.9%
52 How OECD interacts with non-member countries	92	0.3%	96.9%	74.3%
53 Subscriptions to OECD services	90	0.3%	97.2%	75.7%
54 Photos / images / videos	80	0.3%	97.5%	77.1%
55 OECD Annual Forum / Ministerial Council Meeting	73	0.2%	97.7%	78.6%
56 Have your say (public consultation and participation)	71	0.2%	97.9%	80.0%
57 How OECD is funded (budget)	70	0.2%	98.1%	81.4%
58 How peer review works	60	0.2%	98.3%	82.9%
59 Find OECD officials (secretary-general, directors, ambassadors)	59	0.2%	98.5%	84.3%
60 Acronyms, abbreviations	57	0.2%	98.7%	85.7%
61 Personalize the website (MyOECD)	56	0.2%	98.9%	87.1%
62 Press conferences (calendar, accreditation)	56	0.2%	99.1%	88.6%
63 Find a local bookshop / distributor for OECD publications	51	0.2%	99.2%	90.0%
64 Publishing rights and permissions	45	0.1%	99.4%	91.4%
65 What's involved in OECD membership	44	0.1%	99.5%	92.9%
66 Secretary-General speeches and activities	39	0.1%	99.6%	94.3%
67 Find OECD locations	38	0.1%	99.7%	95.7%
68 Tours of the OECD	37	0.1%	99.9%	97.1%
69 Hotels near OECD locations	24	0.1%	99.9%	98.6%
70 Password problems	23	0.1%	100.0%	100.0%

- The tasks at the bottom of the list are not necessarily unimportant. But the top tasks are certainly much more important.
- The number one top task ("Country surveys") received 2,178 votes or 6.8% of the vote. The bottom task, "Password problems", received 23 votes. "Tours of the OECD" received 37 votes. "Secretary general speeches and activities" received 39 votes. The bottom 20 tasks cumulatively received 3.3% of the vote, which is less than half of what the top task received (6.8%).
- Time and time again, we find that tasks at the bottom of the list involve information that the organization wants to tell customers: press releases, senior management speeches, profiles of senior people, annual reports, advertising and branding campaigns, press releases, etc.
- When Liverpool City Council did a Top Tasks survey, they found that far more content was being published for the tiny tasks than for the top tasks. The ego of the organization demanded that the citizens know about things citizens had no interest in knowing about.

- This is what is destroying value in so many digital environments: too much focus on tiny tasks than the top ones. Bloating the website and app—cluttering the navigation, clogging the search—making the top tasks harder to find and more difficult to use.
- This data is no magic wand, but it does often shine a harsh light on the ego of the organization and its often delusional behavior.

Team/stakeholder survey results

If you have carried out a team/stakeholder survey, then you will be able to compare the voting and see if there are differences. Here is an example from an OECD Top Tasks identification in 2009. It shows the type of analysis that can be done. We call it 'Empathy Analysis'—how closely aligned is organizational thinking to customer thinking?

Tasks	% Customer Vote (2381)	% Team Vote (223)	Empathy
Statistics on one particular topic	5.9%	9.6%	163%
Country surveys / reviews / reports	6.8%	5.4%	79%
Compare country statistical data	6.2%	5.2%	84%
Publication by topic	4.6%	5.1%	109%
Statistical forecasts / projections	3.8%	4.7%	124%
Overview of what OECD does	1.2%	4.7%	407%
Browse a publication online for free	5.1%	4.6%	91%
International guidelines and standards	3.2%	4.5%	141%
Basic facts, summaries and overviews	4.3%	4.0%	92%
Statistics on one particular country	4.0%	3.9%	98%

- Empathy will be 100% when the team gives exactly the same vote for a task as the customer does.
- This analysis shows that OECD is in fact quite aligned with its customers. (Much more aligned than we find in many other large organizations.)
- The only serious misalignment is with the task "Overview of what the OECD does", which the team thinks is four times more important than the customer does.

Category question detailed analysis

The detailed analysis touches on the category/demographic questions. Here is the analysis of a question to UK businesses on company size.

How many people are there in your business?

	Percent	Votes
1 - 5	59%	523
6 - 25	23%	205
26 - 250	11%	94
251 or more	6%	54
Don't know	1%	11
	Total	887

The preceding table is sorted by the total column and indicates that there is a lot of commonality of top tasks regardless of business size. (Tasks shaded in grey are top tasks.) We do notice, however, that for those companies with less than five members of staff, "Managing people" is not a top task. This makes sense.

Finding links and connections between tasks

Once you get people to choose their top tasks, you can do all sorts of interesting analysis to discover relationships and connections between tasks. In the UK Business Top Tasks poll, we found the following set up relationships for those who voted for "Tax returns":

Tax returns (complete, amend)

Tasks	Original position
Cashflow, invoicing, payment management	1
Accounting, financial management	6
Calculate tax	24
Tax rates, allowances	27
Pay taxes, duties	21
Check tax liabilities, payments	31
Paying, payroll, taxing staff	19
Records management (tax, staff, environmental)	28
Grants, benefits, entitlements from government	7
Productivity / profitability	3

- Those who voted for "Tax returns (complete, amend)" also had "Cash flow ..." as their number one task.
- However, their number two task was "Accounting" which came 6th in the overall poll.
- Their number three task was "Calculate tax", which was 24th in the overall poll.
- By doing this sort of analysis, we can see the tasks that cluster around or are associated with a particular task.

Full league table of tasks

Produce a league table showing the position of every task. So, if you had 100 tasks in the shortlist, present a league table showing the position of every one of the hundred tasks.

3

Customer Architecture

Seven principles of effective digital navigation

1. Momentum
2. Unity
3. Twins
4. Minimalism
5. Clarity
6. Fidelity
7. Magnetism

Momentum

Design for forward momentum. Designing digital navigation is not that different from designing navigation for a road. You should always help people maintain their momentum in order to get to their destination as quickly as possible. The essence of momentum is to help people move forward, and this is the essential purpose of navigation: to help people move forward.

Yes, there may be some navigation to help people move backward (or 'do a U-turn'), but that should be minimized. You should always assume that the page that person is on is the page they want to be on. How do they move forward from this page so as to get to their final destination? (Assuming that the page they are on is not, in fact, their final destination.)

So, for example, when you select "Musical instruments" on the Amazon website, the vast majority of the navigation becomes focused on helping you choose a musical instrument.

- The search is filtered to musical instruments.
- Most of the horizontal navigation is about musical instruments.
- All the left side navigation is about musical instruments.
- All other products and services have been squeezed into a single link: Shop by Department.

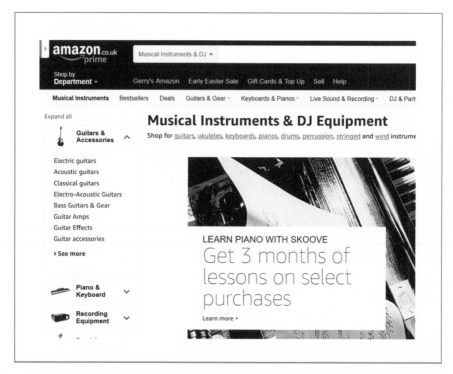

Navigation should help people to maintain forward momentum, to focus on the task. You should trust people that they are where they want to be. If they have made a mistake, they can use search or hit the back button. The job of navigation is to get them to the end of their journey as quickly as possible.

Unity

Navigation should be as unified as possible—kept together in the same screen area. There's nothing worse than having pieces of navigation put all over the place without any real logic as to why. Of course, it may make sense to separate certain types of navigation (login, my account, etc.), but the core navigation—particularly about the products and services—should be as unified as possible.

Disparate, messy navigation is a common mistake, particularly on older websites. Why? The website launches with a poorly designed navigation. Someone tries to fix the problem by adding some more navigation (but doesn't remove the old malfunctioning navigation). Little by little, new pieces of navigation are added, all trying to address specific issues. Before you know it, there's a spaghetti junction of disparate, overlapping, and competing navigational models all over the page and the whole thing is a mess. This is also a very common mistake made by those who don't understand the Top Tasks approach. They add a small section to their website navigation called "Top Tasks". This just adds to confusion and clutter, and it makes the customer experience even worse, as people try and navigate through a hodgepodge of navigation approaches. To reemphasize the point: Top Tasks is an approach for the entire customer experience (including the tiny tasks). If you are not going to use it for your entire online environment, you are much better off not using it at all.

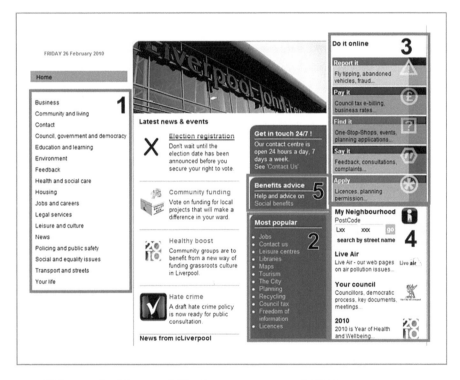

This was the Liverpool City homepage around 2010:

1. This left side navigation was some sort of poorly designed central government initiative. It never really worked, but councils/municipalities were afraid to remove it, so they started adding what they believed were more useful navigation.

2. Such as "Most popular". So, clearly, the navigation on the left side is "Unpopular"? "Most popular" resembles a badly implemented Top Tasks

approach, except that now it's competing with a plethora of other unpopular navigation on the page and contributing to an even more confusing customer experience.

3. "Do it online"? What on earth does that mean to a normal person? Is the other navigation "do it offline"? This, again, was a central government initiative, a promotional campaign to encourage the introduction of online services. However, it got embedded in the navigation of a great many council websites, creating duplication and confusion. And, of course, nobody dared remove it because they thought that there must be a good reason that everybody else was using it. But the reason everybody else was using it was that everybody else was using it.

4. "My Neighborhood"? If you're looking for the library in your neighborhood, will you find it there? No. My Neighborhood was council jargon for a limited set of services.

5. "Benefits advice". Why isn't it under "Most popular"? Why is it on its own? Maybe they forgot to add it to "Most popular", and then didn't have room and had to add it as its own very special little box?

Liverpool City conducted a Top Tasks analysis and then radically simplified its navigation, unifying it and focusing it on the top tasks of its citizens.

'Twins'

After spending years watching all sorts of customers attempt all sorts of tasks, we have noticed certain core navigational patterns emerge. One of the most essential navigational patterns is what we call *twins*. For a great many tasks, there are two dominant journeys (or paths) that customers would like to take. Consider the following tasks:

- Download the latest firmware for the RV042 router.
- Find the waiting times for Child and Adolescent Mental Health Services.
- What is the lowest price service for a 2015 Prius Active?
- Did more people die of heart attacks in Canada than in France in 2010?

People tend to think about the above type of tasks in two ways:

1. From an 'Object' point of view
2. From a 'Subject' point of view

Download the latest firmware for the RV042 router.

- **Object:** I want to get to the RV042 homepage, then look for the firmware to download.
- **Subject:** I want to get to the download software section, then look for the RV042.

Find the costs for Child and Adolescent Mental Health Services.

- **Object:** I want to find the Child and Adolescent Mental Health homepage, then look for costs information.
- **Subject:** I want to go to the costs section, then look for Child and Adolescent Mental Health Services.

What is the lowest price service for a 2015 Prius Active?

- **Object:** I want to get to the Prius Active homepage, then look for service costs.
- **Subject:** I want to go to the Service section, then find costs for a Prius Active service.

Did more people die of heart attacks in Canada than in France in 2010?

- **Object:** I want to get to the Canada or France homepage, then find a link for health.

- **Subject:** I want to get to the Health homepage, then find a link to heart disease and then find information on Canada and France.

Around 2010, OECD had a very convoluted navigation, as can be seen from the following screen-grab of the homepage:

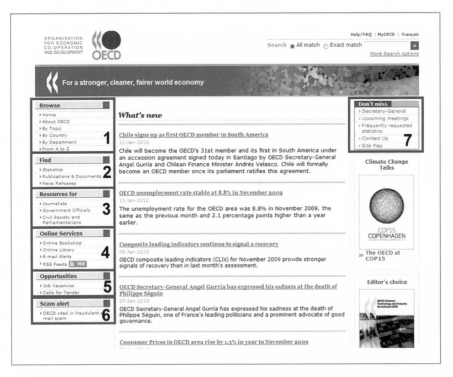

- Along the left side was a whole range of navigation options, including: Browse, Find, Resources for, Online Services, Opportunities, and Scam Alert.
- In the right column, there was a navigational option called "Don't miss". Why did they call it: "Don't Miss"? Just because they know something's wrong with the right column. Here's a tip: if you want people to miss something, put it in the right-hand column. Practically nobody looks there.
- We completed a Top Tasks exercise with OECD and found that there were Twins. OECD customers think about tasks in two basic ways: Countries and Topics. When we showed this evidence to OECD, they changed to the following simplified structure, which very much stresses countries and topics.

Minimalism

The closer you get to your destination, the more you should minimize the navigation. Once someone has chosen to look at the "Martin Smith W-100 Acoustic Guitar", let them focus on that guitar. Make the page all about that guitar. Strip away navigation that is not about that guitar.

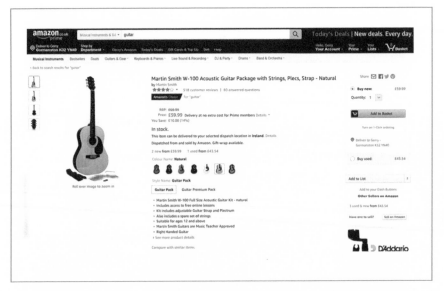

Nobody is at your website or app to gaze lovingly at your navigation. "I didn't like the Grand Canyon itself, but I did enjoy the fonts they used on their signposts," said nobody, ever (except maybe a graphic designer).

Navigation should not draw attention to itself. It should take up as little space as possible while still being functional and helping people get to where they want to. If your customers are spending a lot of time staring at your navigation, that is most definitely a problem. If the navigation was clear, they could quickly scan it and then choose what they needed to do.

Try and keep the navigational space on your page as minimal as possible. Obviously, an extreme example of this would be the disastrous 'hamburger' menu, which hides navigation entirely at the top level of the site. Why was the hamburger such a disaster?

1. Because it used an icon and icons are an awful form of navigation, particularly when they have no words associated with them. So, why do so many sites use icon-only navigation?
   a. Because they look cool. Many traditional designers think words look ugly. If they can't get rid of the words, they'll try to make them as invisible as possible with unreadable grey text.
   b. Because icons save space.

c. Because icons save localization costs. (Everybody in every language gets equally confused.)

2. The hamburger was implemented at the top level of sites in order to channel customers towards promotions, and other marketing and communication initiatives. The idea was to decide for the customer what journey they should go on—not a good idea on the Web.

The use of minimalism does depend on where exactly on the site you are. If you are on the homepage of a site like gov.uk, which seeks to deliver a massive range of services to an entire population, then it can make sense to dominate the page with navigation.

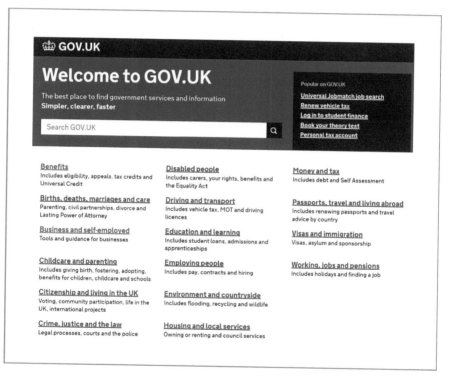

Why? Because the first thing that the vast majority of people want to do when they arrive at such a page is to search or click on a link that will help them continue on their journey to complete the task they came to do. However, once you get to a specific benefit, the navigation is minimized so as to focus on the content for that particular benefit.

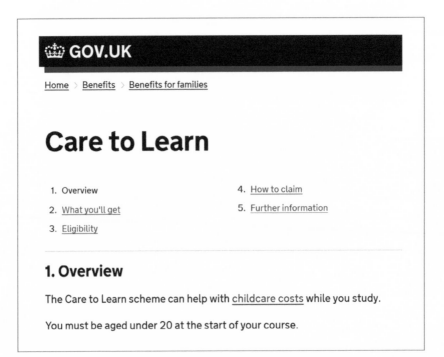

Clarity

From a navigational point of view, what do the following mean to you?

- Resources
- Tools
- Knowledge Base
- Tutorials
- Documents
- Datasheets
- Manuals
- Videos
- Frequently Asked Questions
- Quick Links
- Useful Links
- Do It Online
- Solutions
- Top Tasks

It would be generous to say that they are unclear. Formats are terrible forms of navigation. What is a 'document'? What is not a document? How is a document different from a 'manual'? What is a 'tutorial'? Is a tutorial a document? Is a 'data sheet' a document? And are all these things 'resources'? Most of the aforementioned are print concepts, totally unsuited to a quality digital environment. Instead of data sheets, why can't we say technical specifications? Instead of having documents, have installation, configuration, pricing, etc.

One of the laziest and least useful forms of navigation that grows like a weed on the Web is "Frequently Asked Questions." If someone comes to your website with a question, how do they know it's frequently asked or not? FAQs are one of the worst examples of organization-centric thinking. The organization knows it's a frequently asked question. The customer does not.

Let's say customers are constantly asking about prices. What should you do? Create a link in your navigation called "Pricing", of course. FAQs are the ultimate in design laziness. Instead of actually organizing for the customer, let's just dump a bunch of stuff into an FAQ. (Most of the stuff you find in FAQs are not even frequently asked!)

The following shows a real example (I did not make it up, I promise you) from a website of frequently asked questions gone wild:

- <u>Frequently Asked Questions (FAQs)</u>
- <u>General Frequently Asked Questions (FAQs)</u>
- <u>Customer Service Frequently Asked Questions (FAQs)</u>

"Madam, would you prefer General, Customer Service, or plain old frequently asked questions?"

Tools are a terrible form of navigation. It is an awful approach to separate tools and content. People want to book a flight, not find a tool. And videos? Oh, I haven't seen a video in days. Any video will do. And Solutions? What does that mean? Sure, it's marketing nirvana, but we have seen countless customers get confused and annoyed when they clicked on it. Delivering solutions may be a good strategy but as a form of navigation, it is worse than useless. In fact, it is dangerous because it is a classic example of a dirty magnet, something I'll explain in more detail later.

The best and clearest navigation link is a task. The best link tells you what it is—but just as importantly—tells you what it's not. "Costs" is what it is. "Costs" is not "Schedule". The clearest links often avoid verbs such as "find" or "get". Stripping away the verbs allows you to start with a more unique word. Don't use "Get Pricing". Use "Pricing". Unless the verb is absolutely essential, strip it away. Focus on the essence of the task.

Fidelity

If most links were married they'd be getting divorced, because they never keep their promises. A link is a promise. Navigation is a promise. Don't say "Book Now!" when it's actually five steps to book. That's like saying on a road sign "New York Now!" only to then explain that New York is 80 miles away. It really annoys people. Good navigation gives people a sense of what's involved in the journey: how many steps, how long it will take, what exactly they will get. A link is a promise. Keep your promises.

Magnetism

The magnetism of a navigational link is made up of two elements:

1. Clean magnetism: Its ability to get people to click on it for the tasks it can help them complete.
2. Dirty magnetism: Where people click on it for tasks it can't help them with, but they think it can help them.

A good navigational link maximizes its clean magnetism while minimizing its dirty magnetism. Thus, an overall magnetism score is calculated by subtracting the dirty magnetism score from the clean magnetism score. (I'll discuss this in more detail later.)

Summary

1. Momentum: Keep people moving forward.
2. Unity: Make navigation as unified as possible.
3. Twins: Design for the journeys customers are on.
4. Minimalism: Have navigation take up as little space as is practical.
5. Clarity: Navigation must immediately communicate what it is—and what it is not.
6. Fidelity: A link is a promise. Navigation should keep its promises.
7. Magnetism: Maximize clean magnetism. Minimize dirty magnetism.

Designing a customer architecture

Top Tasks is a solution for the entire set of tasks that your customers wish to complete. The top tasks themselves get priority in this customer architecture but everything must be findable. The tiny tasks will have their place; just lower in the architecture. This is an essential point. Top Tasks is not some add-on to the existing navigation. It is the entire navigation. If you simply add a Top Tasks section to your navigation, then you are likely making the overall customer experience worse.

This method is about discovering the customer journeys and patterns that already exist and then designing a customer architecture around these discoveries. It helps you understand the way customers would most like to see things organized; the words that they most prefer to see used in the navigation. There are always dominant patterns and journeys.

The following steps are involved:

1. Customer sorting and grouping:
   a. Start compiling a list of tasks to sort by first adding the top tasks (those that have received the first 50% of the vote). This is typically no more than 15 tasks.
   b. Add other important tasks such as:
      i. Tasks just outside the top tasks that are seen as important.
      ii. Top tasks of key sub-categories. For example, you might wish to include the top tasks of men and women or of current and potential customers.
      iii. Tiny tasks that have a high management priority, though you don't want to add more than two or three of these.
   c. Keep your list under 30 if possible, and a maximum of 35.
   d. Get at least 15 customers to sort and group these tasks, ideally more than 30.
   e. Identify patterns that emerge and then create a hypothetical classification (a list of "classes" grouping the tasks) from these patterns.
2. Test hypothetical classification:
   a. Create 15-30 task instructions based on the top tasks.
   b. For each of these task instructions, assign a class from the hypothetical classification that you expect people to select to complete the task.

   c. Get at least 15 more customers to decide where they would click on the hypothetical classification if they were trying to solve these tasks.

   d. Success is measured based on whether they have selected the expected class for each instruction. The target is to achieve an 80-90% success rate.

   e. Usually, after the first round, we have a success rate in the region of 60%. Make changes to the classification based on what you have learned (for example changing a class name or deciding that more than one class is correct).

   f. Run the test again.

   g. Typically, it takes three rounds to get to an 80%-plus success rate.

Sorting: Getting customers to group tasks

Choosing the tasks to be sorted

The first step is to get customers to sort tasks into the groups that they think are the most logical. You will select these tasks based on the results from your task identification process. If you have not done task identification, then you need a defensible way to identify the tasks that are most important to your customers and your organization.

Every task that you choose for sorting will have an influence on the overall classification and navigation design. So, you don't want to include too many tiny tasks as they will reduce the emphasis on top tasks in the final navigation.

Typically, we have 50-80 tasks in our overall task-list. We have found that sorting about 30 of these is sufficient to create the foundation for a top tasks classification.

In deciding the number of tasks for the sorting list:

1. Aim for no more than 30 tasks for sorting (maximum of 35).

2. Have no more than 50% of the overall tasks in the sort. So, if you have 50 tasks in the final task-list that was voted on, you should aim to sort no more than 25 of them.

3. If you've got highly engaged and interested customers, then they won't find it much of an issue to sort 30 tasks, but if your customers are not engaged, then aim for about 20.

To compile your list, consider the following:

1. The first 50% of the overall vote. This is typically 12-18 tasks. These are guaranteed to get into the sorting list.
2. The first 50% of the vote for key sub-categories or demographics. So, for example, if current and potential customers are important, then you want to make sure that the top 50% of the tasks for each of these groups are in the list.
3. Tasks near the top of the 50%-75% range of the vote. Let's say that the final top task (in the first 50% of vote) has 1.7% of the vote. The next task (in the 50-75% range) might have 1.6%. That's a reasonable task for inclusion.
4. Tiny tasks (in the bottom 25 percent of the vote) that are seen as strategically important to the organization. These types of tasks should not be over-represented on the list as they begin to shift the classification away from a customer-centric design and towards an organization-centric one. Try to keep them at 10% or less of the final sort list. So, in a list of 30 tasks, there should not be more than 3 of these types of tasks.
5. In certain circumstances, it might make sense to break up a task from the task identification process into two or more sub-tasks to verify that people do indeed group these sub-tasks together. For example, in one sort we had a task called "Procedure and guidelines." We broke it up into: "Procedures;" and "Guidelines," because we wanted to confirm that customers would group procedures and guidelines together.

#	Tasks	Vote
1	EU law, rules, treaties, judgments	5.20%
2	Research and innovation	5.20%
3	Funding, grants, subsidies	5.00%
4	Education and training in EU	3.70%
5	EU strategy, political priorities	2.80%
6	Environmental protection	2.80%
7	Jobs, traineeships at the European Commission	2.50%
8	Find a job in another EU country	2.40%
9	EU news, announcements, press releases	2.30%
10	Human rights, fundamental rights	2.20%
11	Working in an EU country (rights, permits, benefits)	2.20%
12	Order, download an EU publication	2.10%
13	Track policy and law-making process, updates	2.10%
14	Statistics and forecasts	2.10%
15	About the European Union (role, structure, how it works, origin)	1.90%
16	Food and farming (production and safety)	1.70%
17	Climate change, global warming	1.70%
18	Regional, rural and urban development	1.60%

These are the top tasks (the first 50% of the vote) that went into the sort for the European Commission in 2014. Typically, there are no more than 15 top tasks, but this was for the European Commission, encompassing top tasks surveys in 24 languages and 28 countries, seeking to get a statistically reliable understanding of the views of 500 million people. Even with such a huge and complex audience, there were still only 18 top tasks.

21	Product safety, conformity, certification	1.50%
24	Culture (heritage, arts, films, Capitals of Culture)	1.50%
25	Doing business in the EU	1.50%
26	Economic growth, financial stability in EU (crisis, assistance to member states)	1.40%
27	Doing business with the European Commission (calls for tenders, bids)	1.40%
29	Industry norms and standards	1.30%
33	Travel within, to and from EU (documents, visa, consular help, currencies)	1.20%
35	Banking and financial markets (reform, regulation)	1.10%
36	Relations with non-EU countries, international organizations (diplomacy, cooperation agreements)	1.10%
38	Competition (state aid, cartels, mergers, anti-trust)	1.00%
39	Development and humanitarian aid	1.00%
43	Loans, access to finance, microfinance	0.90%
63	Accession of new countries to the EU, enlargement	0.50%

These tasks were either top tasks of an important demographic/category or were seen as strategically important to the European Commission. In total, there were 31 tasks selected for sorting.

How many people needed to sort

- Get a minimum of 15 people—ideally 30 or more—to independently sort the tasks into groups. Our own analysis found that at around 15 people, sorting patterns begin to stabilize.
- Because you're looking for a relatively small sample (15-30), you should aim for no more than 2-3 categories in deciding the participant mix (age, gender, profession, etc.).
- Give people a short survey after they've sorted the tasks to confirm you are getting roughly the right mix based on your categories. Keep the survey very simple. If you're asking about age, then only give a couple of options (under 40, over 40) because you're only going to have about 15 people sorting, so you need a very simplified survey.
- Generally, you don't need to worry too much about sample mix, once you've established certain essential parameters. So, if you're asking people to sort tasks in relation to buying a car, for example, you need to establish that they have some reasonable intent to buy a car. After that, you don't need to be too exact in the sample you get.

The online tool we use for sorting is Optimal Workshop (www.optimalworkshop.com).

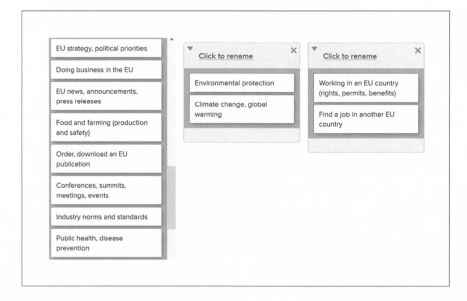

Running a sort

- All the tasks will be presented in a column in a randomized order.
- The person then sorts the tasks into groups.
- Generally, we do make it compulsory to sort everything because that shows a certain commitment from the participant.
- If they wish, they can name their groups, though you should avoid forcing them to do this, as many people find it very challenging to name groups, and when forced, will either abandon the exercise or give very generic names.

Creating a hypothetical classification from the sort

We analyze the data from a sort using a:

1. Similarity matrix
2. Dendrogram

Climate change, global warming						
87	Environmental protection					
52	51	Regional, rural and urban development				
44	44	53	Food and farming (production and safety)			
22	24	30	52	Product safety, conformity, certification		
16	14	21	40 68	66	Industry norms and standards	

In the preceding similarity matrix, "Climate change, global warming" has been grouped together with "Environmental protection" 87% of the time.

In the preceding dendrogram, we see:

- "Global warming, climate change" and "Environmental protection" are tightly grouped together.
- "Find a job in another EU country" and "Working in another EU country" are also tightly grouped, though not as tightly as the previous example.
- "Competition (state aid, cartels)" is not grouped with anything. This is what we call an 'orphan' task. An orphan task is one that stands in isolation. It has not been grouped strongly with any other tasks.

In the similarity matrix and dendrogram, a 50% or higher grouping shows a reasonable relationship between tasks.

Your objective now is to analyze the sort data and identify the key groups/classes and give them names.

1. Aim for less than 10 classes. For very large and complex environments, you might have up to 15 classes.
2. All tasks in the first 25% of the task identification vote should have a place in the top-level classification that will be named after them. The following tasks were in the first 25% of the vote for the European Commission, so they are guaranteed to appear in the top-level classification:
   1. EU law, rules, treaties, judgments
   2. Research and innovation
   3. Funding, grants, subsidies
   4. Education and training in EU
   5. EU strategy, political priorities
   6. Environmental protection
3. In the final design, the above tasks became the following classes:
   1. Law
   2. Research and innovation

3. Education
4. Funding, Tenders
5. Strategy
6. Energy, Climate change, Environment

4. Orphan top 25% tasks absolutely must have a place in the top-level classification.

5. Tasks in the 25%-50% range have a reasonable case for appearing in the top-level classification.

6. Tasks outside the top 50% need to fit under classes already created for the top 50% tasks unless there are exceptional circumstances.

Everything goes into the classification hypothesis

People are great at grouping, but terrible at naming groups. That's your job. Remember:

- It's just a hypothesis. Whatever you come up with you're going to rigorously test.
- All the tasks from the Top Tasks Identification vote must fit into the hypothetical classification that you create. Everything.
- As you seek to classify everything, you may notice that certain tasks just don't fit. You will need to come up with a strategy for how to deal with these tasks.

There were 74 tasks in the Irish Health Top Tasks identification. The following chart shows how the first 30 were initially classified.

TT No	Tasks name	%	Class
1	Waiting times (hospitals, clinics, other health services)	4.9%	Find services
2	Mental wellbeing (stress reduction, mindfulness, positive thinking)	4.5%	Mental and physical wellbeing
3	Costs and fees (treatment, drugs, consultant visits, care)	4.0%	Costs and entitlements
4	Screening (breastcheck, retinal, bowel, cervical)	3.6%	Screening and vaccinations
5	Diagnosis of condition / disease	2.9%	Conditions and diseases
6	Check symptoms / signs	2.9%	Check symptoms
7	Emergencies, what to do	2.8%	Emergencies
8	Health services near you	2.6%	Find services
9	Right place to go for help (GP, hospital, pharmacist)	2.5%	Find services
10	Entitlements, allowances (medical card, GP card, European Health Insurance Card)	2.5%	Costs and entitlements
12	Diet, food, nutrition (healthy eating, intolerances, weight)	2.4%	Mental and physical wellbeing
11	How to use health services (getting the care you need)	2.4%	Find services
13	Access my medical / health records (test results, prescriptions)	2.4%	Find services
14	Living / coping with my condition / disease (support, counselling)	2.2%	Conditions and diseases
15	Detailed information about condition / disease	2.1%	Conditions and diseases
17	Drug effectiveness, side effects, interactions, dosage	1.8%	Conditions and diseases
16	Self-management of a condition / disease (tools, self-monitoring, medicines)	1.8%	Conditions and diseases
18	Appointments (book, reminders, cancel, reschedule)	1.7%	Find services
19	Vaccinations, immunisations	1.7%	Screening and vaccinations
20	Prognosis / likely course of condition / disease	1.7%	Conditions and diseases
22	Confidentiality, privacy, data protection	1.7%	Costs and entitlements
21	Hospital, clinic, health centre opening times, contact details, parking	1.7%	Find services
23	Treatment outcome (immediate, long-term)	1.7%	Conditions and diseases
24	Seriousness of condition / disease	1.6%	Conditions and diseases
25	Exercise (benefits, type, fitness goals)	1.6%	Mental and physical wellbeing
26	Causes of condition / disease	1.5%	Conditions and diseases
27	Risks of being in hospital (hygiene, infections, bugs)	1.5%	Find services
28	Find doctors / GPs	1.5%	Find services
29	Treating minor health problems myself	1.5%	Conditions and diseases
31	Community-based support groups (parenting, carers, counselling, social activities)	1.4%	Find services
30	Patient rights	1.4%	Costs and entitlements

The following chart shows how the bottom 20 were classified:

54	National support agencies, associations for a condition / disease	0.6%	Find services
55	Risk of a specific condition / disease	0.6%	Conditions and diseases
56	Rate, review health services (hospital, GP, pharmacist)	0.6%	Find services
57	Medical equipment (devices, gadgets, aids)	0.6%	Costs and entitlements
58	Environment's impact on health (water quality, radiation)	0.5%	Find services
59	Make a complaint	0.5%	Costs and entitlements
60	Employer health obligations	0.5%	Costs and entitlements
61	Other conditions / diseases linked to a condition / disease	0.5%	Conditions and diseases
62	Preparing for an appointment (doctor, public health nurse)	0.5%	Find services
63	Preparing for hospital / treatment	0.4%	Conditions and diseases
64	Treatment abroad	0.4%	Conditions and diseases
65	Update personal details (address, phone number)	0.4%	Find services
66	News about the health service	0.4%	
67	Sharing medical experiences, stories	0.4%	Conditions and diseases
68	Medical terms glossary	0.3%	Check symptoms
70	Registrations and certifications (birth, death, marriage)	0.3%	Find services
69	Travel health (precautions, vaccinations)	0.3%	Screening and vaccinations
71	Donate or volunteer	0.3%	
72	About the health service (management, objectives, strategies)	0.3%	
73	Track and share lifestyle changes	0.2%	Mental and physical wellbeing
74	Events, conferences	0.1%	

You will notice that there are some blanks near the bottom of the chart. These were mainly organization-centric tasks. It was decided that these would be treated separately in a more corporate-style website, with a link from the footer of the main site.

For the European Commission, there were 77 tasks. Once you've done the initial classification, you will be able to calculate how much of the overall task identification vote each class has received. The following table shows what tasks made up the "About the EU" class, and how they got 12% of the total customer vote.

#	Tasks	%	Class
15	About the European Union (role, structure, how it works, origin)	1.9%	About the EU
19	Freedom of information (transparency, access to documents)	1.6%	About the EU
20	About the European Commission (role, structure, how it works)	1.6%	About the EU
24	Culture (heritage, arts, films, Capitals of Culture)	1.5%	About the EU
37	Languages in the EU (diversity, translation, interpreting)	1.1%	About the EU
41	Contact European Commission, European Union	1.0%	About the EU
46	Euro (coins, notes, eurozone, Economic and Monetary Union)	0.8%	About the EU
53	EU budget	0.7%	About the EU
54	EU vocabulary and abbreviations	0.7%	About the EU
68	Complaints to the European Commission	0.4%	About the EU
72	Visit EU institutions, guided tours	0.3%	About the EU
73	European Commissioner profiles	0.3%	About the EU
77	President of the Commission (profile, agenda	0.2%	About the EU
	Total	**12%**	

Once you've classified everything you can, you will get a table like the following:

Class	%
Business	15%
Work, Live, Travel in EU	13%
Law	13%
About the EU	12%
EU Strategy	7%
Funding, Grants, Financing	6%
EU News, Publications	6%
Environment	6%
Research & Innovation	5%
Education & Training	5%
Food, Farming, Rural	3%
Human Rights, Aid	3%
Jobs at European Commission	3%
(blank)	2%
Grand Total	100%

We see that four big classes have emerged. "Business"; "Work, Live, Travel in EU"; "Law"; and "About the EU" make up 53% of the overall vote. You're beginning to get a feel for what the classification will look like, not just the individual top tasks, but also the top classes. (At the point when this exercise was done, 2% of the tasks had not yet being classed and therefore were labeled "blank".)

This gives us not just an initial classification list, but also the order in which the classes can be presented. It says—based on the data—that "Business" is the most important class for people when it comes to interacting with the European Union.

Testing the Classification

Remember, we just have a hypothesis here. It's our best judgment based on the sorting data of what the classification should look like. Now we need to test it with real people.

Below is an example from Irish Health of a task instruction and the choice of classes. The participant is given the instruction and then asked to select the class they think will help them find the answer.

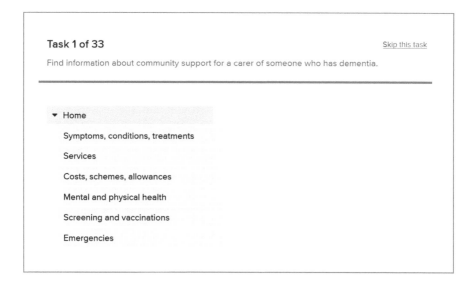

Task instructions

The best way to figure out if your hypothetical classification is working is to give real people real tasks and measure if the classification is helping them head in the right direction.

The task instruction text you will create has the greatest potential of any factor to damage the validity of the findings of your study. The people you ask to carry out the exercise will behave like Sherlock Holmes as they hunt for clues in the text, so we need to get this text right.

Number of task instructions

The first step is to decide which tasks you are going to create instructions for. You should select between 15 and 35 task instructions. It's very important to test at least 15 tasks to see the interactions between tasks and classes. By having a wide range, you may observe, for example, that while a particular class is working well for a certain type of task, it is not working well at all for another type. The number you select will be guided by:

1. Task sort: Ideally, every task that went into the classification sort should have a task instruction.
2. Top Task importance: If a top task is seen as particularly important or complex, it may justify two or more instructions.

3. Problem tasks: As you created the classification you may have found tasks that were particularly hard to classify. These can be good candidates for task instructions.

4. Avoiding too much Tiny Task influence: Remember, as you add instructions for tiny tasks, you are likely influencing the core design of the classification. The more tiny task instructions you add, the more the design is likely to lean towards tiny tasks.

Writing task instructions

1. Keep them relatively simple. You're testing the first click, not the entire journey for a task.

2. Avoid any language that too obviously leads towards the answer. It's a balance between clarity and not being so leading that the answer is obvious.

3. Avoid any words in the task instructions that also appear in the hypothetical classification.

4. Keep the language neutral. Avoid specifying gender, if possible, and avoid using the first and second person.

5. Keep instructions under 15 words and ideally under 10 words.

Here are some examples of task instructions that the Irish Health Service Executive used to test its classification:

- Top Task 1 - Waiting times (hospitals, clinics, other health services): Find the waiting times for Child and Adolescent Mental Health Services.
- Top Task 4 - Screening (breast check, retinal, bowel, cervical): Find out how to get checked for bowel cancer.
- Top Task 5 - Diagnosis of condition/disease: What tests are carried out to check for heart disease?
- Top Task 7 - Emergencies, what to do: If someone banged their head and felt very dizzy, what should they do?
- Top Task 9 - Where is the right place to go for help (GP, hospital, pharmacist): Where should someone go if they have a high temperature and want treatment and advice?
- Top Task 10 - Entitlements, allowances (medical card, GP card, European Health Insurance Card): Apply for a medical card.
- Top Task 13 - Access my medical/health records (test results, prescriptions): How to find results of a blood test.

- Tiny Task 22 - Confidentiality, privacy, data protection: Find the data protection safeguards for personal records.
- Tiny Task 27 - Risks of being in hospital (hygiene, infections, bugs) Check the risks of MRSA (hospital bug) if undergoing an operation.

Here are some examples of task instructions for the European Commission classification project:

- Top Task 1 - EU law, rules, treaties, judgments: Find the VAT directive.
- Top Task 2 - Research and innovation: Find out which scientific and technological fields the EU is promoting.
- Top Task 3 - Funding, grants, subsidies: A researcher wants to start a new project. Find out if there is an EU grant available.
- Top Task 5 - EU strategy, political priorities: What are the EU's top 3 priorities for the next 5 years?
- Top Task 8 - Find a job in another EU country: Find a job in another EU country.
- Tiny Task 18 - Regional, rural, and urban development: Find out what projects the EU is supporting in a particular city.
- Tiny Task 21 - Product safety, conformity, certification: Find the EU requirements for toy safety.
- Tiny Task 24 - Culture (heritage, arts, films, Capitals of Culture): Find out which EU cities are capitals of culture this year.
- Tiny Task 27 - Doing business with the European Commission (calls for tenders, bids): How does a company become a contractor for the European Commission?
- Tiny Task 29 - Industry norms and standards: Find the CEN industry standards for construction materials in the EU.
- Tiny Task 36 - Relations with non-EU countries, international organizations (diplomacy, cooperation agreements): Which agreement is being negotiated between the EU and the US?

Mapping task instructions to a classification

For each of the task instructions, you must now select what you think is the most appropriate class in the classification:

- Top Task 3 - Funding, grants, subsidies: A researcher wants to start a new project. Find out if there is an EU grant available.

Hypothesis (level 1)	
Business	
Work, Live, Travel in EU	
Law	
About the EU	
Strategy	
Funding	████
News, Publications, Events	
Environment	
Research & Innovation	
Education	
Food, Farming, Regional development	
Human Rights, Aid	
Jobs	
Statistics	

So, for the task about a researcher wanting to find out if there is an EU grant available if they want to start a new project, we expect them to start their journey by clicking on the "Funding" link. Do this for all the task instructions and you will then have a full hypothesis to test.

Setting success rate targets

- Minimum average success rate: 80%
- Target average success rate: 90% plus

It is almost impossible to get 100% success in this sort of study. I have certainly not seen it happen. Sure, some of your task instructions will have a 100% success rate, but others will not. If you're testing 30 task instructions, expect to have 2-3 that end up with a success rate somewhere in the region of 60%. Just make sure that none of these are top tasks.

No classification can work perfectly for every task. Once it's working well for the top tasks and once the overall average success rate is above 80%, that's a major achievement. However, you should push to get over 90% if possible.

Getting participants

- You need a minimum of 15 participants to start getting stable data. Ideally, you should get 30 or more.
- Because you're dealing with a small sample, choose no more than three main categories/demographics to segment your audience. For example: Gender; Age; Potential or current customer.
- For a category, choose no more than three sub-categories. For example, if you are asking about age, the following sub-categories would probably be fine: Under 40; Over 40.

The best type of participant is visitors to the website/app. Thus, they are 'fresh' and focused. Subscriber customer lists can also be a good source. As a last resort, use third-party panels or lists.

Analyzing classification results

Bring as many key stakeholders into the analysis process as you can. Once most people can see that decisions are being made based on evidence—on data, and that they have been involved in interpreting the evidence, you are much more likely to get buy-in when you present the final results.

For those stakeholders that you can't involve actively in the process, make sure you have a plan to present to them, not simply the final results, but the step-by-step process that was used to get these results.

It usually takes three rounds of testing to achieve an 80%-plus success rate. After Round 1, we typically get success rates in the region of 50% - 60%. We now need to identify what caused the failure rates and make changes so that when we run Round 2, the success rates will improve.

When analyzing the results look out for the following:

1. Classifications
   a. Are there any wording problems with the names of individual classes?
   b. Is there a class missing?
   c. Is a class simply not working? Is it consistently drawing more than 10% of clicks for instructions it shouldn't be, and not drawing sufficient clicks for instructions it should be drawing clicks for? Does it need to be deleted, or, perhaps, broken up?
2. Task instructions

a. Is something in the wording of the instruction causing problems? Is it unclear or misleading?

b. Has an essential instruction been missed?

You will also want to watch out for the following patterns emerging from the data:

1. Twins
2. Product is the Hub
3. Dirty magnets
4. Weak magnets

Identifying Twins

In the navigation principles, I wrote about the importance of designing for twins. When people are navigating they tend to want to go one of two typical journeys:

1. Object-focused journeys: I have a thing/object. How do I get to the 'homepage' of that object so that I can do something?
2. Subject-focused journeys: I have something I want to do with a thing/object. I'm going to start my journey by looking for that.

Top Task 3: Funding, grants, subsidies: A researcher wants to start a new project. Find out if there is an EU grant available. This question only had a 48% success rate in the first round of testing.

Class	Percentage
Business	1%
Work, Live, Travel in EU	1%
Law	1%
About the EU	0%
Strategy	1%
Funding	48%
News, Publications, Events	0%
Environment	0%
Research & Innovation	48%
Education	1%
Food, Farming, Regional development	0%
Human Rights, Aid	0%
Jobs	0%
Statistics	1%

- The hypothesis was that people would select "Funding". 48% did. However, another 48% chose "Research & Innovation".
- This is a classic example of Twins. Some people think of it as a funding journey. Some people think of it as a research and innovation journey.

This may seem like a simple issue, but it actually has profound organizational implications. Most organizations are organized around disciplines, systems or silos. In the European Union, there is a major discipline for funding. In an ideal world, from an organizational perspective, it would be more efficient for someone seeking funding to come to the funding website. However, the world is a lot messier than that. If we want to make things easier to navigate and improve the overall customer experience, we must ensure that when someone comes to "Research & Innovation", they will see a link for innovation and research funding. Of course, we are not simply talking about this one example here. It will probably be the case that people also think this way for other types of funding tasks too.

Tiny Task 43: Loans, access to finance, microfinance: Find out if an entrepreneur can get money from the EU to help them export to China.

- 46% selected Funding
- 45% selected Business

Tiny Task 43: Loans, access to finance, microfinance: Find out how the EU helps small companies get loans.

- 41% selected Funding
- 41% selected Business

Thus, we have a decision to make. Should we make both twin-type journeys correct? While recognizing that this would require more work and ongoing maintenance from EU staff, it was accepted that it was the right thing to do. In Round 2, it was confirmed as the right decision.

A researcher wants to start a new project. Find out if there is an EU grant available.

- Round 1: 48% success
- Round 2: 92% success

Twins occur in every study we have done. In the OECD, for example, we found a dominant Twins concept of countries and topics. So, when we measured a task such as:

Did more people die of heart attacks in Canada than in France in 2010?

- Some people thought of this as a country task and wanted to first find the Canada or France homepage.
- Some people wanted to start their journey by going to the Health homepage.

In the world of Irish health, we also found lots of Twins:

Top Task 10 - Entitlements, allowances (medical card, GP card, European Health Insurance Card): Apply for a medical card.

Conditions, diseases, treatments	1%	-1
Services	48%	+2
Costs, schemes, allowances	52%	+0
Mental and physical wellbeing		
Screening and vaccinations		
Emergencies		
Check symptoms		-1

Top Task 1 - Waiting times (hospitals, clinics, other health services): Find the waiting times for Child and Adolescent Mental Health Services.

- 56% selected Services
- 37% selected Mental and physical wellbeing

Top Task 5 - Diagnosis of condition/disease: What tests are carried out to check for heart disease?

- 48% selected Conditions, Diseases, Treatments
- 37% selected Screening and vaccinations

While Twins are reasonably common, Triplets are pretty rare, though they do occur. Obviously, you need a very compelling argument to have three customer journeys for a particular task instruction.

The Product is the Hub

If there is one recurring theme that I have found in all the navigation and classification work I have done on web behavior since 1994, it is that a consistent and substantial number of people expect to find the place (the homepage) for the thing (the object) they are interested in. They expect that in this place they will find everything they need to know about this thing. Everything.

- In Toyota, the 'thing is a car like the Prius.
- On a health website, the 'thing' is a disease like cancer.
- On a university website, the 'thing' is a subject like History.
- In Microsoft, the 'thing' is a product like Microsoft Excel.
- In Cisco, the 'thing' is a router like the RV042.

I call this "Product is the Hub." Everything you ever wanted to know about the thing (the object) is here. That's what customers want. It's how a significant quantity of them think. They might have a support issue, but they start off on a product journey. They want to get to the product homepage and then look for downloads or troubleshooting or whatever. What do they find? An organization of silos.

- The product homepage is only for marketing content. It doesn't have any content or links for support or community information for the product.
- Even within marketing, you have silos. The "Promotions" page is managed by its own group and doesn't link or integrate with other pages linked to the product being promoted.
- There is no real support homepage for a product. Instead, there are silo systems for community content, documentation, and weirdly named things like "Knowledge Base".
- The cancer homepage may have a description of the disease and symptomatic information, but it might not have research information, or the ability to find out which hospitals specialize in which cancer treatment.

Once you run these studies, you will be able to quantify the impact of all this sort of organizational 'silofication' and dysfunction. You will be able to show how designing for how the customer thinks, rather than how the organization works, improves findability and the overall customer experience.

Dirty magnets

As I explained in the section on navigation principles, a dirty magnet is something that draws clicks when it shouldn't. People click on it thinking it will help them solve their task, but it won't. Let's take an example:

Top Task 8 - Find a job in another EU country.

Business	1%
Work, Live, Travel in EU	54%
Law	
About the EU	
Strategy	
Funding	
News, Publications, Events	
Environment	
Research & Innovation	
Education	1%
Food, Farming, Regional development	
Human Rights, Aid	
Jobs	44%
Statistics	

In hindsight, the reason for the poor performance of this task was obvious. The "Jobs" classification was supposed to be only for those looking to work within the European Commission itself. "Jobs" on its own was thus too high-level, too all-embracing. While it did work well for the task about finding a job at the European Commission, it became a classic dirty magnet for the other task, getting 44% of the score for those trying to find a job in another EU country. (Another reminder of why it's important to measure a wide range of task instructions.)

The following changes were made:

- Round 1: "Jobs" (44% of dirty magnet clicks).
- Round 2: "Jobs" was changed to "Jobs at the European Commission". Dirty magnet clicks dropped from 44% to 17%.

- The target class was "Work, Live, Travel in the EU". In round 1, it got 54% of clicks. In round 2, it got 79%.
- The problem was not fully solved but things were heading in the right direction.

In the health study, there were also some dirty magnets.

Tiny Task 25 - Exercise (benefits, type, fitness goals): Find out how to get more physically active.

Conditions, diseases, treatments	3%	+2
Services	3%	-4
Costs, schemes, allowances		-2
Mental and physical wellbeing	75%	-13
Screening and vaccinations		-1
Emergencies		
Symptoms and self-care	19%	+19

In "Symptoms and self-care," the words "self-care" were taking on a broader meaning than intended. They were meant to signify the person dealing with minor symptoms on their own. However, they were overlapping with the wellbeing concept in "Mental and physical well-being."

Small word changes can have a big impact. In a technology environment, we changed "Setup" to "Setup and configuration" and there was a 50% improvement in the success rates of relevant tasks. Changing "Account" to "My Account" saw improvements in the range of 10% to 20%. Words matter. Test to see which ones work best.

Weak magnets

A weak magnet is a classification for something that is not being selected when it should be. It has a label that is confusing and unclear. For example:

Tiny Task 18 - Regional, rural, and urban development: Find out what projects the EU is supporting in a particular city.

In Round 1, we only had a 27% success rate. There were two major issues:

1. We had Twins. People thought of it as a funding and a regions/city-type task.
2. The classification "Food, Farming, Regional Development" wasn't working. This was essentially a hodgepodge of very loosely associated tasks.

Business	1%
Work, Live, Travel in EU	8%
Law	
About the EU	6%
Strategy	4%
Funding	37%
News, Publications, Events	6%
Environment	1%
Research & Innovation	4%
Education	1%
Food, Farming, Regional development	27%
Human Rights, Aid	1%
Jobs	
Statistics	4%

- For the next round, the old class was deleted and two new classes were created: Food & Farming; EU Regional & Urban Development.
- As a result of these changes, the task about projects being supported in a particular city increased from a 27% success rate to 83% success in the next round.

Magnetism score

One of the ways of understanding how well your classification is working is by calculating a "Magnetism Score". A magnetism score is calculated based on:

The average success rate a classification has for task instructions

minus

The average failure rate, when it is drawing clicks for task instructions it shouldn't be, and thus behaving as a dirty magnet.

This gives you a sense of which classes are performing well, and which might need some more work.

In the Irish health study, the "Screening and vaccinations" class had a clean magnet average score of 57%.

Tasks Name	Task Instruction	Score
Vaccinations, immunisations	Find out when a child should get the MMR vaccine.	88%
Screening (breastcheck, retinal, bowel, cervical)	Find out how to get a smear test.	58%
Access my medical / health records (test results, prescriptions)	Find results of a blood test.	57%
Diagnosis of condition / disease	How does someone find out if they have diabetes?	25%
	Clean magnet average	**57%**

It had a dirty magnet average score of 6%.

Tasks Name	Task Instruction	Score
Appointments (book, reminders, cancel, reschedule)	How does someone make an appointment for their first scan during pregnancy.	29%
Complications of condition / disease	How do sexually transmitted infections affect fertility?	8%
Diet, food, nutrition (healthy eating, intolerances, weight)	How does a woman know if she is producing enough breast milk for her baby?	5%
Risks of being in hospital (hygiene, infections, bugs)	Find out how to avoid catching the winter vomiting bug in Hospital.	5%
Drug effectiveness, side effects, interactions, dosage	Find out whether mothers can take paracetemol if they are breastfeeding.	3%
Seriousness of condition / disease	How serious is hand, foot and mouth disease?	3%
Living / coping with my condition / disease (support, counselling)	Find information on managing insulin levels for diabetes.	3%
Treatment outcome (immediate, long-term)	After a hernia operation, when can someone return to work?	2%
Causes of condition / disease	What are the causes of emphysema?	2%
Confidentiality, privacy, data protection	Find out how to access your personal health records.	1%
	Dirty magnet average	**6%**

Thus, its magnetism score was 51% (57% minus 6%). In a complex environment, 51% is quite a good score.

Customer architecture: designing with the customer

You will be much more successful if you discover the main journeys that customers are on and design for them. In digital journeys, the roads are built out of words. You are a word engineer. A word researcher. Get the class labels right and you get the foundations right.

Remember, this is an information architecture for **everything**. Top Tasks is not some little section on your website or app. If you're going to follow that approach, it is the road to ruin. You will just confuse and ultimately make a joke of your navigation. Save yourself a lot of time and hassle. Don't do Top Tasks.

The tiny tasks will inevitably come screaming. The ego and the politics of the organization will surely rise up against you. If you've used evidence at every step of the way that can prove that this new customer architecture makes things easier to find; then at least you have a logical, compelling argument. (Logic may not be enough in some organizations.) If you have led people with you at every step of the way, then you are much more likely to get buy-in from these people for this new, evidence-based customer architecture—designed *with* customers *for* customers.

4

Task Performance Indicator

Customer success and time

With the Task Performance Indicator (TPI) you will observe real people attempt to complete their top tasks. You will get reliable management metrics for how successful they are and how long it is taking them.

The purpose of the TPI is to give you an ongoing management metric so that you can say things to management such as:

- In January, we had a 50% success rate and an average time-on-task of 3 minutes.
- We identified A, B and C as the major problem areas.
- We did a lot of work on A, and some work on B and C, costing €20,000.
- Our July TPI shows a 65% success rate and an average time-on-task of 2.5 minutes. As a result of these improvements, support requests have dropped by 10%, resulting in an estimated saving of €15,000 per year. Online sales have increased by 3%, representing a revenue increase of €20,000 per annum.
- We have a set of initiatives in relation to A, B, and C that we believe if fully implemented will raise success rates by another 10% and take an extra 20 seconds off the average time-on-task. We estimate this will result in further cost savings of €30,000 and online revenue growth of €60,000. The estimated costs are €50,000 and the work will take six months to complete.

To allow you to say the above things, the TPI must:

Measure top tasks, not tiny tasks.

1. Deliver a reliable metric for success and failure.
2. Deliver a reliable metric for time on task.
3. Help identify the challenges affecting success and time.
4. Allow for solutions to be proposed and implemented.
5. Be repeatable.

The steps involved in carrying out a Task Performance Indicator are as follows:

1. Decide the key metrics (success and time).
2. Decide what tasks to measure.
3. Select customers.
4. Create task instructions.
5. Develop customer journeys.

6. Prepare measurement environment.
7. Carry out measurements.
8. Make changes based on the findings
9. Measure again to see if the changes increased task success rates and reduced time-on-task.
10. Repeat, repeat, repeat.

Measuring success and time

To measure success rates for tasks we must ensure that:

1. The person undertaking the task knows exactly what is being asked of them.
2. They have the potential to complete the task. In other words, we are not asking them to do something that is impossible—or extremely difficult—for them to do.
3. There is a clear answer at the end of the task so that we know with absolute certainty whether they have completed the task or not.

To measure time, we must know:

1. When the task starts.
2. When the task ends.

In measuring time, the first step is to establish a 'target time'. A target time is the amount of time you expect it will take to complete a task. For example, if you were told that it was taking 280 seconds to "Download the latest firmware for the RV042 router," would that be a good or a bad thing? You don't really know. However, if you had calculated that it should take 40 seconds to download firmware, then you can say that it's taking seven times longer than necessary to complete this task.

Consider the following when calculating target time:

- For most tasks calculate target time based on the expected customer journey that starts at the homepage and uses links to progress through the journey.
- For certain tasks, the dominant customer journey will begin with a search. Calculate these target times by starting with a typical search.
- Once the expected customer journey is established, time a colleague as they search or click through each step of the journey that has been defined.
- Analyze the times that it takes once you have completed the actual measurement sessions. (You don't need to calculate target times before you

run the measurement sessions.) What is the average time looking like? Look at the fastest times. If for example, several people are completing the task in 25 seconds and yet you have a target time of 75 seconds, then you need to question whether you have calculated the right target time.

- The calculation of target time should also be influenced by an understanding of best practice. For example, if you are measuring resetting a password, then you should look to peers/competitors and see how fast it is to do there. This may influence you to set a shorter target time than that which is calculated using the current customer journey.

- Expect that the target time will get shorter over time as new technologies and techniques allow for the further simplification of a task.

The TPI is not so good for measuring:

- Tasks that should be completed within very short target times. This is because it's hard to be absolutely precise about when a task starts and when it finishes. It is thus recommended that the minimum target time for a particular task should be no more than 20 seconds.

- Tasks that have a target time of 2 minutes or more. This is because many people will end up taking much longer than the target time. You expect it will take them 2 minutes but, in reality, many will take much more time because of poor content and design. We find that after 5 minutes at a particular task people begin to lose focus and interest. Therefore, long, complex tasks need to be broken up into more discrete smaller sub-tasks. It is thus recommended that the maximum target time for a task should be no more than 2 minutes.

- When setting a target time round upwards in increments of 5 seconds. So, if you have calculated the target time as 41 seconds, round it up to 45 seconds. This is because it is impossible to get a truly accurate target time and you don't want to be giving the impression of high accuracy with very precise times.

- Over the years, we have found that a typical target time is somewhere in the region of 1 minute.

Here's how to compare the actual time that participants take to complete tasks to the target time:

- If the actual time is less than 1.5 times the target time, do not call it out as a significant issue.
- Only when actual time is more than twice target should you begin to get concerned.
- Any task whose actual time is five times greater than the target time has serious issues.

You don't usually need to worry too much about these times in the first year or so of running TPIs. Your focus is much more likely to be on getting your success rates up. Only in mature environments, does customer time become a relevant conversation topic. Also, as you do more and more measuring, you will develop a deeper understanding of what a target time for a particular task should be.

Measure top tasks, not tiny tasks

Most organizations are obsessed with creating content and launching apps for tiny tasks. These tiny tasks are of major importance to management, but the customer doesn't care much about them. And there are so, so many of them. Consequently, most digital teams are being nibbled to death by an unrelenting army of tiny tasks.

No matter how strong the evidence is, there will always be some stakeholders of tiny tasks who will lobby with management to change the navigation labels in order to upgrade their tiny task to a top position. Tread carefully and diplomatically, but don't give in.

The Norwegian Cancer Society needs to raise funds from the public. It had a website that was flooded with messages asking the public to donate to it. When it asked the public what their top tasks were, it was overwhelmingly about diagnosis and treatment. At the very bottom of the task-league were tasks about donations. The Cancer Society did something radical. It massively simplified its website, focusing on cancer diagnosis and treatment. It removed most of the content connected with donations, particularly from the homepage. It deleted huge quantities of tiny task content and launched its new much smaller site in 2012, which had gone from 5,000 to 1,000 pages. (Typically, a fully implemented Top Tasks approach results in an 80%-plus reduction in content.) In 2013, the Society saw a:

- 70% increase in one-time donations
- 88% increase in monthly donors registered

- 164% increase in members registered
- 348% increase in incoming links
- 80% increase in visitors

Subsequent years have seen equally substantial improvements. Solve the customer's problem, and they'll solve yours. In implementing the TPI, you must measure and improve customer top tasks. If you measure and improve tiny tasks, you are likely making the overall customer experience worse.

Choosing 8-12 tasks for measurement

You must choose the top customer tasks for measurement. Previously in this book, I described the Top Tasks Identification method. You don't have to use this method, but you must have an evidence-based method where you can clearly show what are top tasks and what are tiny tasks. If you can't do this, then the likelihood is you will be nibbled to death by the tiny tasks. In organization after organization, this is the unfortunate state of affairs we have found. The digital team is focused on the tiny tasks because they're new and sexy and cool and because some senior manager has some target or project, or for a million other organization ego political reasons. Meanwhile, the top tasks languish. Top Tasks is about a relentless, obsessional, continuous focus on customer top tasks. True customer obsession is top tasks obsession.

After analyzing over 400 websites and apps (from universities to intranets, from tech companies to health organizations), we have found that between 8 and 12 tasks represent the Top Tasks environment. If you measure these tasks, you get the best possible understanding of the essence of customer experience. If these 8 to 12 tasks are not working well, then you're just not delivering a good customer experience.

Below are the results from the OECD Top Tasks survey in 2009. This sort of top tasks identification data is the basis on which we move forward.

Tasks	Total Vote	% of Total Vote 31800	Cumulative Vote	Cumulative Tasks
1 Country surveys / reviews / reports	2178	6.8%	6.8%	1.4%
2 Compare country statistical data	1960	6.2%	13.0%	2.9%
3 Statistics on one particular topic	1869	5.9%	18.9%	4.3%
4 Browse a publication online for free	1610	5.1%	24.0%	5.7%
5 Working papers	1530	4.8%	28.8%	7.1%
6 Publication by topic	1478	4.6%	33.4%	8.6%
7 Basic facts, summaries and overviews	1379	4.3%	37.7%	10.0%
8 Statistics on one particular country	1285	4.0%	41.8%	11.4%
9 Statistical forecasts / projections	1210	3.8%	45.6%	12.9%
10 Access to raw data	1051	3.3%	48.9%	14.3%
11 International guidelines and standards (corporate governance, tax havens, etc.)	1025	3.2%	52.1%	15.7%
12 Statistical sources and methods	1019	3.2%	55.3%	17.1%
13 What's new (hot topics, recent publications, events)	1004	3.2%	58.5%	18.6%
14 OECD policy advice by topic, country	843	2.7%	61.1%	20.0%
15 OECD Annual Report	784	2.5%	63.6%	21.4%
16 Publication by country	746	2.3%	65.9%	22.9%
17 Best practice in policy implementation	739	2.3%	68.3%	24.3%
18 Publication by title	614	1.9%	70.2%	25.7%
19 Simple, easy-to-understand tables and graphs	613	1.9%	72.1%	27.1%
20 News releases	542	1.7%	73.8%	28.6%

We need to choose between 8-12 tasks that we will then develop task instructions for. The final number of tasks to be measured will to some degree be dependent on the target times for the individual task instructions. We have found that one hour is as much as we can expect someone to concentrate on completing tasks.

We typically find we can measure about 8-12 tasks in one hour, with ten tasks often being the number we end up measuring. If, for example, most of the target times are close to two minutes, then you're probably looking at about eight tasks. If most of the target times are under a minute, then you can probably comfortably measure 12 tasks in an hour.

We have a cutoff limit of five minutes for each task. If the participant goes over five minutes, we gently recommend that that's enough on that task, so we should move on to the next one.

The simplest way to choose your top tasks for measuring is to follow the order of the vote. (Simplest is often best.) As an absolute minimum, at least one task instruction must be created for each of the tasks in the top quartile (top 25%) of the vote.

In the example of the OECD, if we followed a strict ranking order, and we were to choose 12 tasks for measurement, then the following tasks would be selected:

1. Country surveys/reviews/reports
2. Compare country statistical data
3. Statistics on one particular topic
4. Browse a publication online for free
5. Working papers
6. Publication by topic
7. Basic facts, summaries, and overviews
8. Statistics on one particular country
9. Statistical forecasts/projections
10. Access to raw data
11. International guidelines and standards
12. Statistical sources and methods

Some exceptions to this approach include the following:

- Sometimes, the very top tasks (the top one to three tasks) are seen as so important that we need to create more than one instruction for each task.
- It may be that for some of the tasks it is currently not possible to complete them on the website/app. We don't generally choose a task where there is no possibility of success. However, in exceptional cases, where the task is seen as really important, or where you need to prove a point, it can be okay to measure such tasks.
- Lower down the league table can be strategically important tasks that are vital to the future of the organization, and it may be decided by management that these must be measured. However, always make it clear that if we measure Tiny Task X, then we can't measure one of the other top tasks. So, in the above OECD example, if we chose a task lower down the table, we would probably not be measuring "Access to raw data". Don't select more than two of these strategic tasks. Otherwise, you undermine the whole Top Tasks approach.

Deciding which tasks to require instructions is an incredibly important step. Key stakeholders must be involved. You must get broad buy-in and sign-off at the most senior level. If you don't do that, you can be guaranteed that it will come back to haunt you later. People will keep challenging you: "Why did you choose that task? Why not this task?" Remember, you are building the foundations here. If you do it right, you will be measuring the same basic tasks in five years' time. Everything flows from the decisions that are now about to be made. Here's what the results of this step might look like within the OECD environment.

OECD Top Tasks	Qs
Country surveys / reviews / reports	2
Compare country statistical data	2
Statistics on one particular topic	1
Browse a publication online for free	1
Working papers	1
Publication by topic	1
Basic facts, summaries and overviews	1
Statistics on one particular country	1
Statistical forecasts / projections	1
Access to raw data	1
Total Task Questions	**12**

As you can see, it was decided that the top two tasks were so important that they should have two task-instructions each. The two task-instructions that were created for the number one customer task, "Country surveys/reviews/reports" were:

1. What are the OECD's latest recommendations regarding Japan's health-care system?
2. In 2008, was Vietnam on the list of countries that received official development assistance?

Becoming familiar with the environment to be measured

Once you've selected the tasks that you're going to develop instructions on, you must become thoroughly familiar with the website or app within which they reside. This may not be an issue for you if you are working on the website or app every day. But even here, it may be the case that you know some parts of the site very well, but other parts you are less familiar with.

- The more familiar you are with the task environment, the more likely you are to create quality task instructions.
- When the actual measuring starts you will have a much better perspective on what is happening. If a participant behaves in a surprising way—and that happens a lot—you are less likely to get confused and unnerved if you know the overall environment very well.

Selecting customers to measure

You will need 13-18 people to attempt the tasks. 13 should be seen as a minimum. Aim towards 15-18 as an ideal. Why these numbers? The following chart explains.

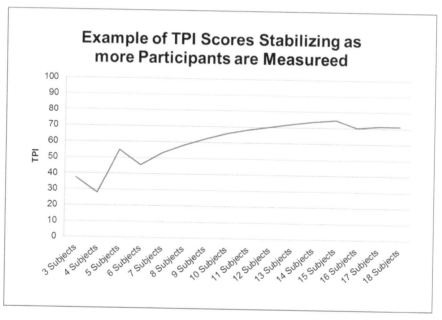

We have found in measurement after measurement that results for a particular task begin to stabilize after measuring about 13 people. What this means is that after you have measured 15 or more people, you can have a high degree of confidence in the stability of the success rate and time-on-task. In other words, your figures will be generally reliable.

Select a representative sample of your customers. Here are the key factors to consider when selecting:

1. **Importance:** How important are they to the organization? Focus initially on the most important customers.

2. **Usage:** How often do they use the website/app? How familiar are they with your products and services? Get a mix. About half who are experienced and half who are less experienced. Or if there's a big difference between the behavior of experienced and non-experienced people then you might need to consider separate TPIs for them.

3. **Role:** In some TPIs, the professional role can be very important. For example, in a Business-to-Business (B2B) technology website, we might have marketing/sales people visiting, as well as technical experts. If there's a big difference between roles you might need to consider separate TPIs. For example, giving marketing tasks to technical experts may not make sense and vice versa.

4. **Top Tasks:** The customers you plan to measure must share all or most of the same top tasks. For example, if current customers have very different top tasks to potential customers, then you will need one TPI for potential customers and one TPI for current customers.

5. **Location/language:** Each TPI is done in one language, so whoever is measured must be fluent in that language.

6. **Gender:** This can sometimes be important.

There are usually no more than two or three profile factors that are really important when deciding who to measure. If you try to have too many factors, then it becomes almost impossible to get the right mix. Don't tie yourself up in knots in relation to getting a very precise mix. If you, for example, know that 50% of male and 50% of female customers come to the website, then if you're measuring 16 people, you aim for eight men and eight women. But it's ok if you have nine women and seven men, or vice versa. You always require some flexibility but don't veer too far from your targets.

Take your time in deciding on the mix because the mix should not change as you continue your measuring over time. So, if you decide that it needs to be 50:50 infrequent customers and regular customers, then that's the mix you need to keep using in the future when you run the next TPI. **This is a very important point.** Changing the mix of your measurement group can affect the TPI scores in an artificial way. So, for example, if the next time you run the TPI the profile is 80:20 frequent customers to infrequent customers, your score might rise simply because you have more people doing the tasks who are more familiar with the environment. (Of course, you're not measuring the exact same people, again and again, just the same profile/type of people.)

Getting people

- If you have run a task identification survey, then you should have used the last question as a request for participants.
- Popups requesting participants, although annoying, are still more effective than simply making a request on a webpage.
- Your organization may well have a list of customers that you could possibly contact.
- Consult people within your organization who interact with customers (sales, support, etc.).
- You can hire a list from a third-party commercial entity. However, avoid this. We find that the people you get from these commercial services are often less interested and engaged. These are often 'professionals.' They do a lot of this sort of stuff and are therefore not a typical customer.

Recruitment, rewards, scheduling

When you have agreed on the profile, you need to screen potential participants to ensure that they meet this profile. You may already have some profile information on them. However, even then, it's good to have them fill out a short profile questionnaire. Over the years, we have found that the profile information we initially get is not always accurate. You don't want to discover in the middle of a session that the participant does not actually fit the profile you have on them. So, you need to confirm with the person that they indeed are who you think they are.

When you are communicating with a potential participant you will need to inform them of the following:

- The profile you have of them and a request to confirm or amend.
- Who will be carrying out the measurement session (you or someone else)?
- The measurement will occur remotely—from their home or office using their own computer. Specify the meeting service to be used (Webex, GoToMeeting, etc.).

- If they will be doing the session from an office, ask them if there are any security restrictions in relation to using proposed service.
- The session will take about one hour. Provide some proposed dates and times.
- Explain that they will be asked to perform a series of pre-defined tasks that they will be given as the session unfolds. (Do not send the task instructions in advance as some people will 'cheat' and try the tasks out in advance.)
- It is not them being measured but rather the website/app.
- They will get a specified reward, typically about $75 (as of 2018). We use Amazon gift vouchers, which are very handy.

Creating task instructions

For the top tasks you have selected, you will now need to create task instructions that you will give to the participants. Each task instruction will take about two hours of work to research and craft.

Start with the answer, not the instruction

Rather than giving an instruction and then looking for the answer on the site/app, browse the site/app and try and find specific information related to the top task you want to measure. Then, see if you can frame an instruction around this specific information.

A top task for OECD customers was "compare country statistical data." We began looking at the comparative data sets. We found a set of health data that compared countries based on mortality rates for various diseases. Then we came up with the following instruction/question:

Did more people die of heart attacks in Canada than in France in 2004?

We knew the answer existed because we had the data set. We also had information on the expected customer journey to the answer.

As a rule, there must be an answer to the instruction on the website/app. In rare circumstances, you may have a top task that cannot be completed on the website/app, but you still want to see what journeys customers take.

Representative, typical, fixable

Select task instructions that are typical of the top task in question. This is not an exam. Do not try and choose difficult, unusual, once-off-type tasks. They should be ordinary, basic, common.

The top task of customers visiting Cisco.com is downloading software. This was such an important task that we measured several types of download tasks. Here's one of them:

Download the latest firmware for the RV042 router.

This is a popular router, and the download process for it is reflective of many other routers that Cisco sells. We didn't choose an unusual router with a unique download process. That's not the purpose of the TPI. Don't look for exceptions. Don't try and be clever. Choose a typical, standard example.

Consider the ability of the organization to fix whatever problems may be identified. Ideally, you want to create task instructions that the web team has some control and influence over. If there is no way to fix the problems, then you're going to be getting the same results every time you do the measuring. That will be dispiriting to the team. Much more energizing is to have tasks that they can do something about, tasks where they can show progress.

Of course, this will not always be the case. There may be a task that the digital team currently has no control or influence over. If you run the TPI and show a high failure rate, then that may be a burning platform for change.

Repeatable

If the TPI is just a once-off project, then you've wasted a good bit of time and effort because you probably could have run a simpler set of usability measures, with fewer people, and found the same basic results. The whole purpose of the TPI is that it is an ongoing management process. Top Tasks is the way you work, the way you manage. It's a philosophy and an approach.

As a result of measuring Task X, you discover it has a 60% failure rate. You feel that A, B, and C are the main causes of this failure. Great. But that's only the beginning. You now need to make sure something gets done about A, B, and C. **Then you need to measure again.**

When you measure again you find the failure rate has only dropped to 50%. It's still much higher than you predicted it would be. It may well be that actually, D is the real cause of task failure but that you overlooked that. That's okay. That happens. It may be that the fix for A has actually made things worse. That happens too. However, the fixes for B and C worked really well.

TPI is about helping you validate your decisions through customer use. It is design through use, management through use. Evidence-based decision making based on how your customers are behaving. To do this you must have repeatable tasks.

In 2009, we measured this task for the OECD:

In 2008, was Vietnam on the list of countries that received official development assistance?

In 2013, we measured this task:

In 2012, was Vietnam on the list of countries that received official development assistance?

We just changed the year from 2008 to 2012, but the essential nature of the task remained the same.

Measuring the same tasks allows you to answer this crucial question:

Are we getting better?

"Repeatability" creates a management model. Repeatability is the essence of what the TPI is about.

For years, we've been measuring this task with Cisco:

Pretend you have forgotten your password for your Cisco account and take whatever actions are required to log in.

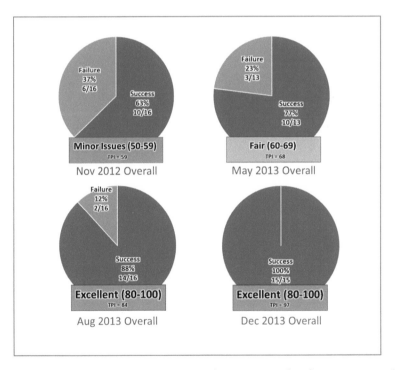

In 2012, it had a 63% success rate, but as a result of continuous effort from Cisco, by the end of 2013, it had reached a 100% success rate. Job done?

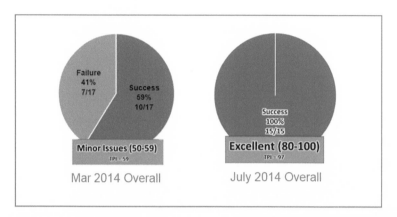

When we measured results again in March 2014, the success rate had dropped to 59%. A technical error had occurred that caused a major drop in success. It was quickly fixed and by July 2014, according to the TPI, the success rate was again 100%.

Digital is never done. You have to continually keep measuring your top tasks. Digital is not a fixed environment. Things are always changing, things are added, things are taken away, the network evolves. Changes that are made in one part of your website or app can have unforeseen effects on another part. You must keep measuring the top tasks.

Avoid giving clues – Anti-Search Engine Optimization

Every single word of every instruction that you give to a participant should be examined and scrutinized with the intensity of a Sherlock Holmes. People will hunt for clues in the text. They will take phrases—or even try to cut and paste the entire instruction—into a search engine. (Do not let them cut and paste instructions into a search engine!)

The instruction is simply noise in an experiment whose ultimate purpose is to understand normal customer behavior. The instruction is unnatural, alien. You are trying to create as natural and normal an environment as possible. The text in the instruction is the single biggest potential pollutant in this whole process. (The next biggest potential pollutant is you!) Badly worded instructions will not just ruin a TPI, but they can also result in false information, bad data, misleading metrics. Because of a badly worded instruction, you can think A is the problem with the task, when in fact the problem is D. So, getting the wording right is incredibly, incredibly important.

Let's say a top task on an intranet is finding policy information. Let's say there is a policy on the intranet called the "Maternity Leave Policy." If you want to see if people can find policies, then what do you think of the following question?

Find the maternity leave policy.

It's not a good question, is it? It contains the phrase "maternity leave policy." Perfect for searching with, and that's exactly what they'll do. Or they'll scan the navigation looking for "maternity leave." This is why your instructions must be "anti-search-engine-optimized (SEO)". Usually, you create content on the Web with people in mind, using words and phrases in your content that they are likely to search for. But when you create a task instruction you need to do the opposite. You need to strip your instructions of any sort of keywords that might easily lead someone to an answer.

Here's a better way to phrase this instruction:

Your colleague is pregnant. How many months can she take off?

If the survey participant immediately searches for "maternity leave," that's fine. It was their choice of search phrase; you didn't lead them to it.

Whenever you have come up with a draft instruction, search with all of the instruction text, and then with key phrases from the text. If the correct page is coming up in the first three results, then change the text. Keep changing the text until it stops bringing up good results.

Be specific: one task, one unique answer

What do you think of this sort of instruction?

Find the dimensions of Product X. Place an order for it.

The first task is to find the dimensions of Product X. The second task is to place an order for it. Supposing the person finds the dimensions but can't place an order. How do you mark the task? We might say that the technical information is well laid out but the ordering process is very poor. However, the ordering process is probably more complicated than getting technical information. Combining tasks into one instruction should be avoided. It creates all sorts of complexities.

It's always better if there is just one place on the website/app that contains the answer. The fewer places there are to find an answer, the more likely you are to identify specific customer journey patterns. If people can find the answer in lots and lots of places, then they can go in lots and lots of directions, and their chances of finding the answer are very high. You don't learn all that much from this type of instruction. The more specific you are, the more you learn.

Here's an instruction from NetApp:

What is the maximum raw capacity for an FAS2552?

This is a good instruction because it has a very specific answer: 518 terabytes. It sounds counter-intuitive, but you learn more about general issues of search and navigation by measuring specific instructions than you do by measuring general instructions, such as "Find some storage products." Another advantage is that with a specific instruction you can more precisely measure the answer. For vaguer instructions it becomes harder to define the answer (How many are "some"?).

Independent and different

Task instructions need to be independent of each other. For example, you shouldn't have to do Task 5 before you can do Task 6. The reason is that you need to be able to change the sequence in which you ask tasks in order to avoid learning that may occur when tasks are always asked in the same sequence. For example, if you always ask in a sequence 1-10, then tasks 8, 9 and 10 might perform better because the participants have learned a good deal about the website doing tasks 1-7. To avoid this possibility, it's better to randomize the order in which task instructions are given.

Don't use task instructions that have the same basic challenge and customer journey. Let's say you have this task instruction:

Find out who is head of Marketing in Germany.

It would not be a good idea to measure this other very similar task:

Find out who is head of Human Resources in the United States.

Two issues occur if you create similar type tasks:

1. The participant learns. Once they've performed the first task, they're likely to do better on the second one.

2. The participant is likely to get a bit irritated being asked the same type of task again. You always want the participant to be in an emotionally neutral state.

Short and clear – 30 words or less

The shorter the better. Aim for less than 20 words if you can for each task instruction. Remember, this will be the first time the participant will see/hear this instruction. (Never send instructions in advance, because some people will 'cheat' and try and do the tasks ahead of time.) You should paste it into the text box of WebEx or GoToMeeting and read it out, or else get them to read it out.

Make it as clear and simple and short as possible. Otherwise, they may forget and have to go back to reread the text. Or worse, they may misunderstand or pretend they understand and go about trying to solve a different type of task (This is one of the key things you want to watch out for when you do a dry run pilot of the task instructions).

Target time: a two-minute maximum

The target time is the time you expect it will take the participant to complete a task. Let's say you have a target time of 60 seconds for Task X. After the sessions, you find that the average time it took people to complete Task X was 4 minutes. You know you have a problem.

We recommend a target time of between 30 and 90 seconds, and certainly no more than 2 minutes. In an ideal world, you should aim for all your tasks to have the same basic target time so that all tasks have the same level of difficulty.

We chose the 30-90 second range for the TPI for the following reasons:

- They are shorter tasks: Do not create task instructions with target times under 20 seconds because they are harder to time accurately. It is difficult to decide with absolute precision when a person starts and ends a task, and this lack of precision affects time calculation for shorter tasks much more than for longer ones.
- Do not create task instructions with target times that are longer than two minutes. Such tasks require a lot of mental effort and increase the likelihood that participants will get tired, frustrated, or distracted. In reality, many people will spend much longer than the target time in trying to complete the task.

- One hour is the total time that most people can spend carrying out tasks with a high degree of attention and focus. We have a five-minute cut-off time for tasks. So, after five minutes, if someone has not completed the task, we politely suggest that they move onto the next task. This means that even if we hit the five-minute limit for most tasks, we can still get about ten tasks tested in one hour.

Other characteristics of good task instructions

1. **Universal—everyone can do them:** This, of course, connects up with participant selection. If, for example, you're measuring a mixture of novices and experienced people, then you don't want to be creating complicated tasks that only an experienced person would be able to complete.
2. **Emotionally neutral:** Keep the instructions boring and neutral. No humor, no talk about a financial crisis, or accidents, or anything that might cause an emotional response.
3. **Not confidential:** People can get quite sensitive about their personal/ company information. Ideally, where personal information is involved, it is better to set up test accounts.
4. **Immediately doable:** Avoid tasks, if possible, where the participant has to wait for an email verification response, for example. Try and ensure everything that needs to happen happens within the environment you are measuring.

Customer journeys for task instructions

Once you have established the task instructions, you need to illustrate in visual and text form their expected customer journeys. These are the journeys that you believe the customer will most likely take when completing the task. Here is an example customer journey from NetApp:

Top Task 3: Data protection

Task Instruction: Find a document that gives you the ten key benefits of NetApp SnapVault.

Expected Customer Journey:

1. NetApp.com homepage
2. Click on 'Products' in the Products Mega Menu

3. Click on 'Data Protection Software'
4. On the 'NetApp Data Protection Software' page, click on 'SnapVault'
5. On the 'SnapVault' product page, go to 'More info' on the right-hand side, then click on 'SnapVault Top Reasons PDF'
6. Answer: 'Top Reasons – Why Use NetApp Snap Vault Replication-Based Disk-to-Disk Backup' PDF

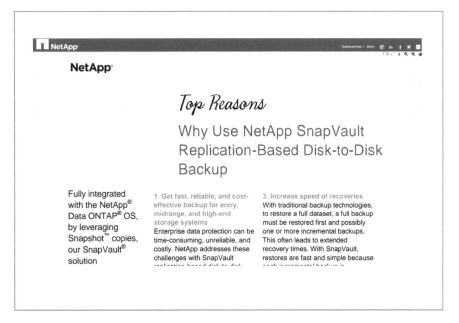

Here's a customer journey for a UK government business support website:

Top Task 1: Cash flow, invoicing, payment management

Task Instruction: You have a debt owed to you of £2000. It is overdue since the 1st of June 2011. You have no contract with the debtor. You can charge interest. How much?

Expected Customer Journey:

1. http://www.businesslink.gov.uk/
1. Finance and grants
2. Debt recovery
3. Calculate the interest due on an unpaid debt
4. Go straight to the first question

5. Statutory interest
6. When was the contract formed? (any date in the first six months of 2011)
7. When was the principal debt paid (leave blank)
8. When did the payment first become overdue? (enter 2000)
9. Are you a public sector body? (no)
10. How many employees do you have? (any number)
11. How many employees does the debtor have? (any number)
12. To be consistent with the other example you should have a **Landing page here with the link**
13. Answer is £123.56

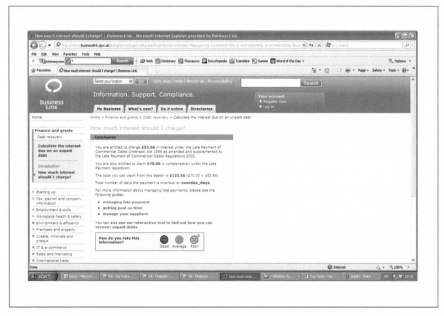

We also usually show an image of the answer. Sometimes, we might show images of each step in the journey. The purpose of developing a customer journey is:

1. For the person who will be carrying out the measurements to get a better understanding of the task we are measuring. If you don't have a clear sense of where you expect people to go to find the right answer, then it's hard to see patterns. It's hard to determine whether they are clicking on expected or unexpected links.

2. It also very important for the person measuring to have an URL and image of the correct page/answer so that they can confirm that the customer being measured has got the right or wrong answer.

3. Target time: A key way to get a measure of target time is to walk through the expected customer journey with a timer.

The customer journey is nearly always defined from a navigational point of view rather than a search one. The reasons are as follows:

1. From observing thousands of customers trying to complete tasks, we have found that in the region of 70% of them will start their task with a navigation attempt. (This is when we start the task on the homepage of the website/app in question.)

2. Even when they use the search function, it tends to send them to a lower level of the customer journey, and from there they will navigate through the rest of the journey.

3. It's very difficult to predict what words and phrases people will use in a search for a particular task. However, if we find a search-dominant task, then we will create a customer journey that begins with search.

Create a customer journey for every task instruction and then put them all together into a presentation or document format.

Deciding where each task starts

Where should each task start from? This is a key decision. For consistency of measurement, every task that you measure needs to start from the same place. There are typically two options:

1. A blank tab: Assuming that it is a web-based task, then a blank tab in a browser is the most optimal place to start.

2. The homepage: Less optimal, but often more practical.

The problem with the blank tab approach is that many participants will immediately head to Google; and for many tasks, they may never even get to the website/app being measured. This, of course, is a useful initial lesson, but you probably don't need to do a full TPI to discover that.

The homepage is imperfect, but you have a much bigger chance of getting a more substantial understanding of how the site works or doesn't work. It really depends on the maturity of your environment. The more mature and well-designed it is, the easier it is to start from a blank tab. But if you're dealing with an immature environment, it's probably better to start on the homepage because you need to learn as much as you can in order to improve things.

As your environment matures, you may decide to move to the blank tab starting point, but that will mean starting the TPI process from scratch. This is because, a success rate score will differ when measured from the homepage, instead of from a blank tab starting point.

The starting point that you establish is simply that—a starting point. You must stress to the participant that for measurement purposes, this is where we will start each task. However, if they want to go use Google as a starting point, for example, no problem. They can do exactly what they want to do from this starting point. The reason we do this is that we seek to create as natural an environment as possible. We want success and failure rates to be as real as possible. We want real times and real experiences.

Measuring

What the person running the session will need

For the person running the task measurement sessions, the following will be required:

1. It is highly recommended to have two screens attached to your computer: One where you observe the customer as they go about trying to complete the task that they have been given; another one where you can make notes, record times and success/failure rates, copy the next task instruction for pasting into the chat box, etc.

2. A tool to record all the start and end times, success and failure rates, and make important notes on your observations as the participant tries to complete the task. At the most basic level, you need a word processor or spreadsheet, but if you're going to do this a lot you're going to need some sort of custom tool that can calculate times, and record and process success and failure information.

3. A Facilitator Guide — a step by step description of everything that needs to happen during a measurement session, including everything you need to say to the participant.

4. A Customer Journey document/presentation. We usually keep the customer journeys separate from the Facilitator Guide. In fact, we usually print out the customer journeys so that we can easily reference them during the measurement session.

5. A service that will allow for sharing screens and recording of screens and voice. We have found the most reliable to be WebEx or GoToMeeting.

6. Video-editing software that will allow you to create video highlights of the sessions.

The Facilitator Guide

1. Welcome the participant.
2. Confirm with the participant that it's okay to record the session.
3. Request for the participant to share their screen.
4. Inform them how long session will last.
5. Give a clear explanation that you are measuring the website, NOT them.
6. Test to ensure they can see the chat box.

7. Agree on a start page for all tasks.
8. Inform them that they can go anywhere they want after the start point—use Google, whatever.
9. Tell them they can't use bookmarks or paste task instruction text into a search engine.
10. Ask them to read each task out loud after it has been pasted into chat box.
11. Tell them they must indicate that they are starting the task.
12. Tell them they must give a clear answer after completing the task.
13. Instruct them to go back to the start point after each task.
14. After last task, ask them for two or three things they liked and disliked about the website/app.
15. Ask them for any final comments.
16. Thank them and inform them when they will be getting their reward, where appropriate.
17. Include a section containing the task instruction list.

Marking a task

It's critical that you mark tasks as correctly as possible because this affects the core success and failure rates, and the times. If possible, have two or more people involved in the marking process. You must get marking as accurate as you can. Imagine standing in front of management and saying that there is a 50% failure rate for a certain task. Then, when others analyze your results they find that you didn't mark certain participants properly. That will seriously undermine your credibility. If you don't have the resources to have more than one person involved in the marking, then do not stress the numbers when you're delivering the results. Instead of emphasizing a 30% success rate, talk about a very low success rate.

Starting the task

1. Always remind the participant at the beginning of every task that they need to inform you when they are starting because people tend to forget.
2. Even when they tell you they're starting, do not start the timer until you see their cursor move because there is often a delay between when someone says something and when they actually start doing it.

Observations

1. These should be brief notes of key behaviors and patterns that you see occurring.
2. A first recommended observation is whether they have started the task by searching or navigating.

Success/completion

1. Success occurs when:
   a. A participant verbally gives the answer. "It's 17%."
   b. They clearly point to the answer. For example, they clearly point at the 17% figure.
   c. It is **not** a success just because the person has arrived at the page where the answer is located. We often see people arrive at the correct page only to leave it again. They may also give the wrong answer after having read the page.
2. Based on your customer journey information you will have an agreed success point.
3. Be aware that there may be other ways of achieving success that you had not expected. Always double and triple verify successes. If at all possible, verify successes with another colleague.
4. **Not marking successes correctly undermines that whole Task Performance Indicator approach.**

Fail

1. If the participant gives up, mark that as a failure.
2. If the participant goes over the time limit (usually five minutes), mark that as a failure.
3. If the participant gets the wrong answer, mark that as a failure. But double- and triple-check that it is actually the wrong answer.
4. **Not marking failures correctly undermines that whole Task Performance Indicator approach.**

Skip

1. Mark a task as a 'skip' when a participant:
   a. Already knows the answer.

b. Misunderstands the task even after several explanations. Someone might seem to understand the task but then go on a totally different journey and start searching for wholly unrelated terms — mark that as a skip.

c. Requires you to explain the task multiple times. If they keep asking you questions during the task, if they're constantly going back and re-reading the task, mark that as a skip.

d. Encounters serious technical problems that are caused from their side. If the problems are caused by your website/app, then the task is marked as a failure.

e. Is interrupted. If they get a phone call during the task or get significantly interrupted by a colleague—mark that as a skip. If the interruption only lasts a couple of seconds, that's usually okay.

f. Is significantly distracted by something you have said or done.

g. Refuses to do the task.

What the person being measured will need

1. A device which they can use to access the website/app. You need to think about the device that the person will use. Basically, they should be allowed to use whatever device they want. However, you may hit some technical constraints, particularly if they wish to use a smartphone, in that the software you use for sharing screens and recording may not work so well with their mobile. Sometimes, you may have a specific objective to measure the differences in task success if the person is using a larger screen versus a smaller one. In this instance, you would need to select participants accordingly and inform people that they are expected to use a certain type of device.

2. The ability to use the software for screen-sharing and recording. You will need to make sure that if you intend to use, for example, WebEx, that they can use that. You need to verify this in advance. Sometimes, if a person is carrying out the measurement from work, then there may be security restrictions, so you need to make sure that everything is working properly.

3. Language skills. International websites may have a dominant language, often English. Lots of people visiting may not be native English speakers. Find out when contacting people whether they have a native, professional, good, or basic knowledge of the language being used for the measurement session. You may find that, for example, those with basic language skills will not be suitable for measuring.

Skills required to measure

The perfect skill set involves being analytical, methodical, empathetic, curious, and especially being a trend/pattern spotter. If you've done usability testing before, where you have observed people as they used a website or app, that's a great start.

Empathy is about being able to walk in the shoes of the person who is attempting the tasks — trying to think like they think, trying to understand why they are doing what they are doing. Your greatest skill is to be a pattern finder, a trend spotter. Your greatest attribute will be to look for the boring stuff that keeps happening again and again. Top Tasks is in many ways the anti-cool, anti-sexy, anti-latest-trend approach. It's about you identifying that:

- Yes, poor metadata is really hurting findability.
- The content you are analyzing is too long, bloated and confusing and needs to be rewritten.
- The links are poorly written and full of jargon.
- The design, while being 'sexy', cutting-edge, 'interactive', and 'innovative' is actually quite useless. You're looking for the underlying causes of task failure and slow task times.

Your first job is to collect evidence of what the underlying causes of failures and slow times are. So, try not to jump to conclusions too quickly. A common problem in this area is that you already have a solution in mind, or some patterns that you've seen before, and you're just looking for evidence that confirms your views. You must keep an open mind. Observe and analyze as a neutral researcher. Recommendations can come later – during the session, stick to fact-finding.

You need patience: Watching 15 people seek to complete a task can be boring for some people. If you get bored very easily and have a short attention span, then this profession is not really for you. It's more for methodical, organized people who are willing to roll their sleeves up and work through the detail.

These are huge skills for the present and for the future. We have all this Big and Small Data on what customers are doing. We need lots of skilled professionals who can understand this data, who can analyze the customer behavior and clearly identify the important patterns and trends.

What NOT to do during a measurement session

Empathy can be a double-edged sword. You need to be empathetic without being too helpful. You need to be empathetic and yet invisible. You want to be the fly on the wall, not the fly buzzing around the participant's head. Be careful that you make as little noise from your side as possible. The less you talk, the better.

For reliable metrics, we must create as natural an environment as possible. The person you are measuring should forget you are there once they start a task. You must never guide or intrude or interfere or suggest unless it is essential to do so. Staying quiet is often the hardest thing for empathetic people to do. You want to help, but if you help you risk ruining the measurement.

It's all about calm, professional invisibility. You have to ignore your desire to help. Even if someone asks you for help with a task, you must politely decline. If someone keeps asking you how they are doing, you can say something like:

"You're doing fine. Everything you do is really helpful to me. It's all great data. So, whatever you would do as you normally go about this task, that's exactly what I want to see."

Here are some specific things to avoid when facilitating a TPI session:

- **No 'talk out loud':** It is common practice in usability to ask people to talk out loud, explaining their way through the task. Do not ask the person to do this. It affects what they will do. Talking out loud for the vast majority of people is not natural. If you ask them to talk aloud then you are getting unnatural behavior. Top Tasks is about measuring what happens in the real world, in the ordinary day-to-day life of the customer. No talk aloud. (Of course, if the participants start talking aloud on their own initiative, that is their choice.)

- **No exception spotting:** This is the classic trait of the amateur. 'Oh, that's interesting! I've never seen anyone do that before. I'll definitely report on that.' Identifying, designing and creating content for exceptions is the opposite of the Top Tasks approach. It is the Tiny Tasks approach. You are really looking for dominant trends and patterns that are affecting a minimum of three or more participants.

- **No guidance, no hints:** The worst possible thing you could do is say: "Why don't you try the search function?" Or: "How about looking over there in the left-hand navigation?" We are aiming for a real-world measure of what people are actually doing when trying to complete a task.

- **No ongoing conversation:** Keep as quiet as possible. Do not engage in an ongoing conversation or banter about weather, politics, etc.
- **No moods:** Keep your voice neutral. Don't sound particularly encouraging or negative. Yes, be friendly, but don't ever say something like: "Wow! That was a hard task" or "Wow! You did really well there!! Got it in no time at all!!!" Don't! Be polite, be professional, but above all be invisible.
- **No judgment:** Some participants will want to know how they are doing. Maintain the same polite approach regardless of whether they are completing every task quickly or failing miserably. Do not become a judge in any way. Never inform them how they are doing. Tell them that everything they do is extremely useful to observe. Now and again, when you see them failing at several tasks in a row, and you sense they are getting frustrated, you might offer a few words of encouragement, such as: "Everything you do here is really helpful. Remember, we are not measuring you. We are measuring the website. For me, you cannot fail."
- **No answers:** If the person really wants to know the answer to a task they've just attempted, tell them at the very end of the measurement session.
- **No background noise:** You don't want anything in your background creating a distraction. Turn off phones, close doors, etc. Do not run a measurement session from a noisy room with lots of people in it. Make sure that your audio setup does not create any echoes or other unusual sounds when you or the participant are speaking. It is important that both of your voices come across clearly. You will also be editing videos of the sessions that many people in your organization may well see. We have found that such videos can have a particular impact on the thinking of senior management, so you want the audio to be as clear as possible.
- **No loud typing:** You will be typing notes during the session but try to be as quiet as possible. Ensure that your microphone is positioned in a way that it picks up as little noise as possible from your typing. Consider muting yourself after you have presented the task instruction and the person has started the task.
- **No loud breathing:** Watch your breathing, particularly if you're wearing a headset. If you get your mic in the wrong position, then your breathing can become really intrusive and irritating. This is something you won't

notice from your side, so you need to do an initial test with a colleague to ensure that breathing and typing are not disturbing the participant.

Measurement sessions

Measurement period, number of observers

Typically, it takes about two weeks to measure 13-18 people. (An entire TPI takes about six to eight weeks.) You'll be very lucky if you get all your sessions done in a week because there's nearly always cancellations and re-scheduling. When planning, ensure that there will be no major changes to the environment you're measuring during the measurement period. Otherwise, you won't be measuring like-for-like, and you will undermine the accuracy and validity of your data.

In an ideal world, there should be two people doing the measurements. So, if you have 15 TPI sessions to do, one person does eight, and the other person does seven, for example. The benefits of having two people doing the sessions are that you will be able to share insights and crosscheck each other. You might mark something as a success that the other person marks as a failure. You discuss and come to a consensus view. You might spot what you think is a common problem/pattern. You discuss with your colleague to see if they're seeing it as well. Your colleague checks your notes and how you've coded things and you check their notes.

It's good to get other key stakeholders involved in observing these early sessions, and, if possible, to have people observing throughout all sessions. However, if you are getting other stakeholders involved in the actual sessions, keep the following in mind:

- They should not in any way communicate with the participant under-taking the tasks unless in very exceptional circumstances. (For example, in technical environments, the instruction may need more explanation that the facilitator can give.)
- They should not communicate with the person facilitating the session unless they have something really important to say. Otherwise, they should wait until the session is over. If they do have to communicate, they should use the chat box.

- Ideally, they should be hidden from the participant. It can be disconcerting for someone to see a list of people who will be watching them as they go about attempting tasks.

Dry run/pilots

Plan for a pilot with a couple of participants to iron out any unforeseen circumstances, particularly in relation to the clarity of the questions. If everything runs smoothly, then you can count these participants as part of the overall measurement. If not, you make the changes required as a result of the pilot and then launch the full measurement sessions. (If this is your first time doing something like this, run several sessions with your colleagues to get the basics right.)

It is particularly important to get extra insights during the pilot phase of measurement and after the first couple of proper measurements. (After that, it's usually sufficient to get together after every two or three sessions.) Things that should be asked:

- Are the instructions clear?
- Are sessions being completed in the allocated time?
- Are people finding answers in unexpected places?

One of the things to particularly watch out for during the pilots is the task wording. For example, a top task for Asian Development Bank (ADB) customers was to find the latest list of proposed/upcoming projects. The task instruction we initially came up with was:

Find the page where the latest ADB consulting jobs are listed.

Some mistook this task for being about getting a job with the ADB and went to the Careers section.

The task was reworded as follows:

Find the page where the latest ADB consulting contracts that organizations can bid for are listed.

Capturing measurement information

You will need a way to capture what the participant is doing during the measurement session. There are two ways to do this. The first is through a video recording of the session. The second is through documenting the session by writing down essential information.

We have created a tool and a process to capture such vital information.

The first step in relation to writing down essential information is to create an individual file for each person who will be attempting the tasks. It's recommended to have a standard file-naming convention. This helps with organizing and processing the information later on.

We would name the above file as "ADB-03GM":

- ADB is the name of the organization that the measurement is being carried out for.
- 03 is the number of participants who have been involved in the sessions so far. So, this is the 3rd session.
- GM are the initials of the participant who is attempting the tasks.

What to say at the beginning of the session

A script for this will be included in the facilitator guide. When the participant who will be attempting the tasks joins the online meeting:

1. Greet them, giving your name and the organization you work for.
2. Inform them that you will be recording the session, but that the recording will not be made public. Then you should start the recording process. Then ask for their permission. It's important to start the recording before you ask for permission so that you have a record of them giving their permission. If they don't give permission, end the session.
3. Inform them that you will soon be asking them to share their screen. Ask them if they want to close anything of a personal nature on their device. Give them time to do that and confirm with them that it's ok to request them to share their screen.
4. Send them a request to share their screen. Confirm with them that they have in fact shared their screen by indicating what is on the screen. Sometimes, people are working with two screens and they share the wrong screen with you. That's why it's good to confirm this.
5. Inform them that the session will take about an hour and is voluntary. They can stop at any moment they want to.
6. Stress that you are measuring the website/app, not them. It's hard to convince people of this as people tend to think that it is their skill that

is being tested/measured. One thing we have found that helps is to tell them that if they want to give up on a particular task at any time, they should do so, that we really learn a lot if we can identify the points where people are giving up.

7. Ask them to open a browser and ask them to maximize it if it is not maximized, as this will give better recording quality.

8. Assuming that the start point for the tasks will be the homepage, post the link for the homepage into the chat box for the meeting tool. This tests whether the person can find and read what is in the chat box. Ask them to click on the link and inform them once you see the homepage appear in their browser.

9. Inform them that while they will start each task at this start point, they can then go wherever they want. They can use Google, for example.

10. Tell them they are not allowed to use bookmarks or shortcuts. The reason we don't allow bookmarks and shortcuts is because we want to measure the standard environment that a typical person faces when trying to complete such tasks.

11. Tell them they can't copy and paste the task instruction text into a search engine. There may be exceptions here. If the task contains a long serial number for a product, and if they need to enter the serial number as part of the process of completing the task, it's ok to allow them to copy the serial number. Also, if it is a ZIP or postal code. Basically, if they need to input data during the task that is in the task instruction, it is better to recommend they copy and paste it because this eliminates the chance of error when entering the data.

12. Tell them that you will soon paste the first task into the chat box, that you will read it out for them but that if they prefer to read it themselves, to let you know. You need to find an approach that they are comfortable with but you must ensure, as far as possible, that they truly understand what is being asked of them.

13. Inform them that once they are ready to start the task, they should say something like "starting now." Explain that you need to know this because you need to time the task. You will need to constantly remind people to tell you this, as they always forget.

14. Tell them that they will need to inform you of the answer when they have completed the task. That you need to know this in order to get an end time for the task.
15. Ask them if they have any questions. If they've no questions, you're ready to go. You can paste the first task instruction in.
16. This introductory phase to the session should take less than ten minutes.

Measuring a task

1. Paste the task instruction into the chat box. Once you're confident that the person understands the task, ask them to inform you when they're ready to start.
2. Even when the participant says they're starting, it doesn't always mean they are. We usually wait until we see the cursor moving after they have said they're ready before recording the start time.
3. Optional: Note whether they are navigating or searching, particularly whether their first action was navigation or search.
4. Whenever they search, try and note the words they are searching with.
5. Note other key observations as the task progresses.
6. When the participant has completed the task, make sure that they clearly speak out the answer to you. Stop the timer after they have given the answer.
7. Ask them to return to the start page. Do not paste in the next task until they have returned to the start page.

Key observations

Here's the type of things you're looking for:

- Are they going along the expected journey or a different one? Remember, you're not looking for exceptional behaviors. Once three or more people start doing the same thing, then you've got a pattern.
- Are they searching or navigating a lot?
- If they're searching, are they using the site search or Google? What type of terms are commonly searched for?
- Do they come to a page, scan up and down it, and then in frustration, go to search? If so, what words are they using? The words that they use can indicate what they were expecting to find on the page.
- Are they on a page where there is a link to the next step, or where the answer is, but they still end up going to search?

- Are they confused by the search results because of poor metadata or out-of-date content?
- Do they use the Back button a lot? Do they arrive at a page, spend ages scanning up and down it, and then hit the Back button?
- Are they doing a lot of frustrated scrolling?
- Is it clear that they are misunderstanding certain content or links?
- Are they systematically scanning the navigation? If it's a mega menu, are they using their cursor to scan back and forth across the navigation?
- Are they clicking on Link A when they should be clicking on Link B?
- Are there speed issues? Do you get any indication that they are frustrated with page load times?

After the final task instruction

1. Thank them for participating. Tell them you've learned a lot.
2. Ask them to tell you about two or three things the site/app does well, and two or three things they think could be improved.
3. Thank them again and inform them that they'll be getting their reward soon (if they have been promised a reward) and end the session.
4. Take time to go over your notes after each session. Did you get your start times and end times right? Did you code things properly (particularly the answer)? You must double-check—and triple-check—your scores.
5. If there are two of you doing the measurements, then you will need to have planned meetings where you will discuss the results and double-check the marking. Remember, Top Tasks is a management model. Your numbers must be accurate.

Video capturing

You need to be able to capture as high a quality video and audio as possible. A carefully edited video of three or four participants struggling at a specific point in a task is one of the most powerful ways to communicate the true customer experience to a wider audience. Seeing the data is one thing. But seeing real customers—one after another—fail and matching that with data is a very powerful combination. Imagine you standing in front of a senior management meeting saying:

"We have a 60% failure rate on this task. The biggest cause of failure is a section of the registration form. I'd like to show you a video of 4 customers failing at this point. What you are about to see is a representative sample of what we estimate to be 600 similar failures a day happening. The support costs alone are estimated to be $10,000 a week. We estimate that lost sales are in the region of $100,000 per week."

Therefore, you need the video to be as high a quality as possible. It doesn't have to be Hollywood quality, but when you project it on a large screen it needs to be clearly visible what the customer is trying to do. If they should speak, then their voice should be as clear as possible.

This is something you most definitely need to test in advance. You will need:

1. A tool to capture video in a standard format that will allow for later editing.
2. A video-editing tool: You will need to be able to cut up the videos and add snippets together from various participants. We currently use Camtasia for this.

Analyzing, presenting, using results

Compiling scores, identifying opportunities

Here are the key metrics you'll need:

- An overall score for the success rate averaged across all tasks. You need a similar score for time. These are your key scores.
- Success rates and time-on-task for each individual task.
- As an option, consider providing information on whether people navigated or searched at the beginning of a task.

The success and time scores are essential. They are the foundation for the Top Tasks Management model. They are the benchmark against which you will judge future work and initiatives. However, what is equally essential is that you identify the causes of the failure rates and the slow times and propose actionable solutions for them.

What are the key customer journeys that have emerged and how do these differ from the journeys that were originally defined? Are there elements of the environment that are causing problems regardless of the task being attempted? What are the 2-3 most important areas for improvement on a task-by-task basis?

Presentation summary

1. **Task instruction selection overview:** Explain how the top tasks were identified — you might use a table for this from the task identification process. Show a table with the top tasks and their respective task instructions.
2. **Participant profile:** Details on who was measured, what was their professional role, where were they located, what size of company were they from, etc.
3. **Overview video:** A summary of three minutes or less of the most powerful feedback from customers attempting the tasks.
4. **Historical performance:** If this is a repeat TPI, then a chart showing the performance over time of success/failure, and time-on-task.
5. **Overall results:** A chart showing average success, failure, and time-on-task for all tasks. A similar chart, if available, for navigation and search options.
6. **Peer comparison chart:** A peer comparison chart, if available, showing how these results compare with similar organizations.

7. **Key overall issues and recommendations:** A series of slides explaining the top two or three key overall issues with clear instructions on how to fix them. Use video and lots of screen grabs. For example, one slide will show a typical customer at a certain page, with a red box around a link, and a statement: "Customers typically clicked here." Then another red box around a different link on the page will have a caption saying: "But we expected them to click here." Show the journeys. Visualize! Identify those core patterns that occur across multiple tasks.

Individual task findings

This will be the bulk of your presentation. Typically, we start with the worst performing task. The slides should include:

1. **Success rate and time on task:** The success rate and the time on task for this task.
2. **Expected customer journey:** The task instruction text and the customer journey that people were expected to take.
3. **Historical performance:** How this task has performed over time, if this information is available.
4. **Issues and recommendations:** Clearly illustrate with screen grabs and video the two or three most critical issues affecting performance. Make precise recommendations on how to fix them.

Presenting video

If you measure 15 people, then you will have 15 videos. This is potential gold for developing an organization-wide empathy for the customer experience. However, the chances of getting lots of your colleagues to watch these videos in their raw, unedited state, are not great. Right now, what you have in your hands more closely resembles coal. Here's how you turn it into gold.

Task-by-task videos

Let's say you have 15 videos and that each person did ten tasks:

- Create a folder for each of the tasks and a final folder called 'Comments'.
- Chop up each participant video by task and place these into their respective folders.

- Let's say that there is a task measuring downloading software. Create a folder called "Downloading Software" and place into it the video section for each participant attempting that task.
- Cut the video into segments at each point where a task instruction is being read out so that each task can be clearly identified. It's very easy for things to get mixed up when you're dealing with 150 video edits (15 people X 10 tasks).
- Typically, end each video at the point where the person gives the answer. If the person spontaneously says something after they've completed the task about their experience, capture that as well. But there's no point, for example, showing them as they head back to the start point.
- Cutting up the videos makes the job of analysis and spotting trends much easier. You can focus on one task at a time and really dig into it.
- Now you can also do a workshop with the download software team and all the other teams. (In larger organizations, different teams tend to be responsible for different tasks.) You can send them the videos in advance, and they are much more likely to look at them because they know that the only footage in these videos relates to the downloading of software. You might also start the workshop by going through the videos.

Video highlights

A video highlight is usually three or more customers struggling at a similar stage in a customer journey. Generally, keep your video highlights under three minutes, ideally under two minutes. Now and then, it can make sense to show just one customer go through an entire journey. In this case, it could be five minutes or more. You introduce it by saying that this happened to lots of customers, that it should have taken less than one minute to complete this task, but that customers went beyond the time limit point of five minutes. You let the video play; and as it goes on and on you might interject: "I know this is taking a long time to watch, but consider the time so many of our customers waste every day trying to complete this task."

Other examples of video highlights include:

- An overall summary of key comments people have made during the measurements. I often introduce my results presentation with this sort of video. "Have a listen to your customers and the experiences they've been having."

- Customers clicking on the 'wrong' link when they get to a certain page. In the customer journey you defined, you expected them to click on a different link on that particular page.
- Customers clicking on the first search result for a particular search even though that result is really out-of-date.
- Customers scanning up and down a page and constantly missing the answer to the task, and then hitting the Back button or using the search function.
- Customers trying to search with your own search engine, not getting good results, then going and searching with Google and getting much better results.
- In selecting and preparing video highlights:
- Have three or more customers in the video if possible all attempting to do the same basic thing.
- Focus your video highlights on the top problems of the top tasks. If you have only time to show one video, then it should illustrate the top problem with the top task.
- Have general problem videos as well as task-specific ones. So, you might have a video showing five customers failing at search across five tasks, then you can say: "Poor quality search is affecting a whole range of customer top tasks."
- As stated earlier, keep the videos under three minutes, if possible, ideally under two minutes.

Example of an individual task-finding

When we surveyed OECD customers in 2009, their number 4 top task was browsing an online OECD publication for free. We came up with the following task instruction:

What is the title of Box 1.2 on page 73 of OECD Employment Outlook 2009?

Essentially, if they got to page 73, it proved they had found the free online publication. Here's how we presented the results for this task. The first slide was the overall results:

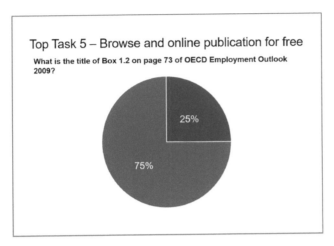

There was a 75% failure rate, which was very significant. The next slide was the expected customer journey:

Expected Customer Journey

- OECD homepage
- Click: Topic
- Click: Employment
- Click: Publications and Documents
- Click: Publications
- Click: OECD Employment Outlook 2009
- Click: Get this book
- Click: Online Bookshop
- Click: Look Inside Eye icon
- Find page 73
- Previously you had the landing page link at this point.
- Answer: Broad reductions of employer social security contributions as a support to aggregate labour

The next slide was for key findings:

- Nobody had any major problems getting to the Employment Outlook homepage. For this initial part of the journey, search and navigation worked well.

- On the Employment Outlook homepage, there were a series of confusing menus and links that led people in the wrong direction. Most people failed to get beyond this page successfully.
- Of those who did click on the expected link ("Get this book"), they also got confused by the links on the Online Bookshop page.
- Of the few who got to the document itself, there were problems finding page 73 because of PDF pagination issues.

Then we showed a typical journey that people took using screen grabs, notes, and recommendations. Here's how it went.

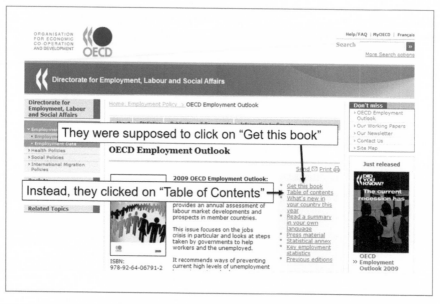

We showed what happened when people clicked on "Table of contents".

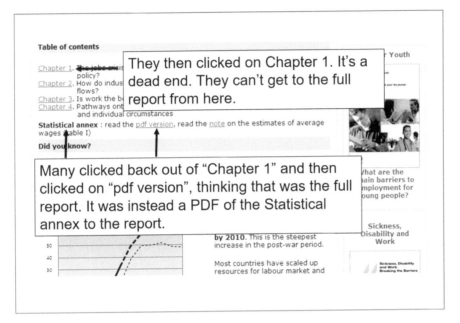

It's confusing menus and links, again and again and again. The boring stuff that so few ever want to address and fix. However, it is this basic, boring stuff that has a huge impact on the customer journey and experience. It is this basic, boring stuff that increases failure rates and time-on-task.

You need to ask what the purpose of the table of contents section is. Is it a tiny task that is disrupting the journey of a top task? Shouldn't there at least be a link to the full report from the table of contents?

When participants failed to find a way to the full report in the table of contents, they then typically scanned around and saw the link "pdf version". When they clicked on it, they got to the "Statistical Annex". This is a classic problem. Where possible, links should not be the format, but rather the destination. The link should not be "pdf version", but rather "Statistical annex (PDF, 2 MB)". Customers try and fit things into the journey they are going on. They're looking for the 2009 Employment Outlook, then they see "pdf version" and they think: "Ah, maybe that's the PDF version of the 2009 Employment Outlook". (PDFs are generally a terrible idea, by the way. They are digitized print content, not digital content.)

This is a specific task with a specific problem, but you have a universal recommendation:

Recommendation: Link text must always start with the destination, not the format. A link is a promise. Tell people exactly what they'll get when they click on the link.

Customers wasted a lot of time in the table of contents section. However, most did not give up but instead went back to the top of the Employment Outlook page and clicked on "Get this book", as we had expected them to do in the first place. Then the real problems began:

Get this book

Readers can access the full version of the OECD Employment Outlook 2009 by choosing from the following options:

* Subscribers and readers at subscribing institutions can access the online edition via <u>SourceOECD</u>, our online library.
* Non-subscribers can browse or purchase the PDF e-book and/or paper copy via our <u>Online Bookshop</u> or order it from your <u>local distributor</u>.
* Government officials with accounts (<u>subscribe</u>) can go to the "Books" tab on OLIS.
* Accredited journalists can access it on our <u>password-protected site</u>.

Permanent URL: <u>www.oecd.org/els/employment/outlook</u>

This section totally confused people. They were supposed to click on "Online Bookshop". But that seems rather counterintuitive, doesn't it? If you want to read a free online version of a report, would you click on "Online Bookshop"? Many gave up at this stage. After reading this section, some said: "There is no free version. You have to pay for it." In measurement after measurement, we have also found that embedding links in sentences nearly always confuses people.

Recommendation: Do not put links in sentences. Write links in the same way you write a heading.

We gave an example of how this section might be rewritten:

<u>Subscribers and readers at subscribing institutions</u>
<u>Government officials with accounts</u>
<u>Accredited journalists</u>
<u>Non-subscribers: browse online version for free</u>
<u>Non-subscribers: purchase a copy</u>

While most gave up or failed at this stage, some did manage to click on "Online Bookshop and reached the next step.

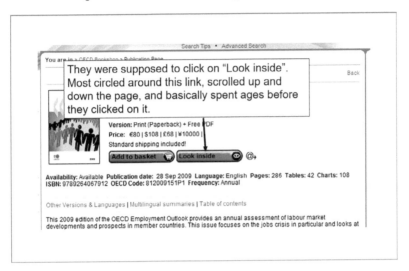

The "Look inside" link was obviously not clearly worded. Some new text needs to be tested for this link. For those lucky few that did click on the link, they got to the PDF document. Most of those used the search function to search for page 73.

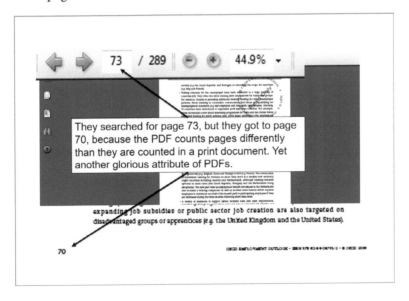

However, they got to page 70! That's because the PDF counts the cover and other introductory pages as pages, whereas a print document doesn't. Okay, PDFs totally suck for most content, and this is just one more nail in the coffin. But do you see how much practical stuff you learn from this sort of measurement process?

OECD started trying to improve things. In one instance, they experimented by adding a link underneath the book image called "Browse this book", which leads you directly to the report.

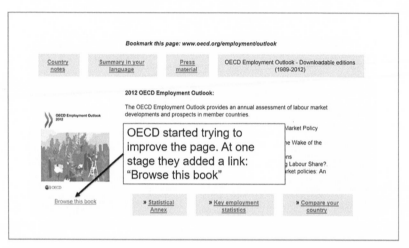

When we measured again, the success rate went from 25% to 100%. Now, you don't often find that sort of dramatic improvement. However, it's true that it's often the small, boring stuff that is most negatively impacting the customer journey and experience. Top Tasks delivers you practical evidence of what is happening, what the customer is actually doing. What the real customer journey and experience is like.

Continuous improvement

Top Tasks is a management model for the continuous improvement of the customer experience. It aims to reduce failure rates and reduce time-on-task. To do this you must be measuring and improving the top tasks on a continuous basis.

Developing a Task Performance Indicator schedule

Your measuring schedule should be based on your capacity to make changes. So, for example, if you're able to implement the recommendations that resulted from a measurement session within a three-month timeframe, there's nothing stopping you measuring again in three months to see how the changes have worked. However, there's no point in measuring again if you haven't implemented at least some of the recommended changes.

Here's something very important to understand. Every day you should be observing the customer experience. The TPI is just one method. Its purpose is to deliver more formal management metrics. But you can run micro observation sessions on micro parts of the task journey. For example, let's say that TPI showed that a particular form is causing major problems. Laser focus on that form. Make changes, then observe three to five customers try and use the new form. Constantly iterate the form based on this sort of feedback. Always be observing and improving.

In the early days of TPI, you will find that quite a few of the recommendations are easy to implement. Your success rate might jump from 50% to 70%, for example, as a result of such changes. But then you start to hit the harder, deeper, structural, or cultural problems. These problems can take a lot of time, effort, and money to fix. There may be software problems that require you getting a new system. But also, cultural work practices and habits can be the hardest things of all to change.

Many organizations, for example, have a quick and dirty approach to publishing content, putting it up on the website in PDFs, with very poor metadata. There's very often no review-and-remove policy, so over time, out-of-date content builds up. The content itself is often written in a vague and jargonistic way. All this will affect customer success rates and time-on-task. Fixing these sort of problems requires a significant cultural change in how the organization views content, and then it requires extensive training and ongoing management. These are not things that happen quickly. However, for the first time, you will have metrics on the impacts of poorly managed content. You'll be able to say things like:

- It's causing a 40% failure rate.
- The average time-on-task is nearly three minutes when it should be less than one minute.

That's no magic wand, of course. Consider it a small torch in a large, dark room. You're throwing some light on the real customer experience. The more measuring you do, the more light you will shed. Have no doubts, this is a long and difficult journey. Even though you are doing the right thing, your organization will often resent you for it because you are the bringer of bad news, and because you're recommending that the organization invest more time and money in actually improving the customer experience. Now, most organizations will enthusiastically say they're all for a great customer experience. Except that they don't want to pay much extra for it, and they don't really want to make the cultural changes that would make them a truly customer-centric organization.

Making people responsible for tasks

If you want to maximize the chances of success, then make employees responsible for customer tasks. That's really hard because it involves changing job profiles and how employees are measured.

It's easy to measure employees based on what they produce or on how many hours they spend at work. That's the old model and it is the root cause of so many awful customer experiences. A technical writer writes a technical description of how a feature works and then publishes it to the website. Job done. Was it findable? Who cares. If it was findable, was it usable? Who cares. In the old model, nobody cares once it is published.

With Top Tasks, the technical writer is not measured based on what they publish but rather based on whether the customer can find, understand, and use what the writer has published. The Task Performance Indicator measures the world from the customer's perspective. It measures the outcome, not the input.

- Has the customer completed the task?
- How long did it take them?

But traditional organizations don't measure customers, they measure employees:

- Has the employee completed the task of writing and publishing the technical description?
- How long did it take them?

That approach sucks. In the traditional organization mindset, the PDF with no metadata is great because the employee completes their task in the fastest possible time. They're a great 'put-it-upper'. From the Latin, *put-it-uppo*, a put-it-upper is someone who churns out lots of low-grade content and designs and puts them up on the website or app as quickly as possible.

What you're trying to introduce with the Task Performance Indicator is a new balance. You're showing the other side of the equation. Yes, you might say, publishing the PDF is faster for the employee, but it is much slower for customers to complete their tasks if they have to find and wade through a big clunky PDF.

What's the cost? The Task Performance Indicator gives you a model where you can begin to measure the cost of a poor customer experience. Imagine a perfect customer-centric world for a moment. An employee sits down with their manager for their performance review. "Well, done, Jean," their manager says, "You've improved the success rate of your customer tasks 10% more than the targets we had set. The time-on-task has also dropped from an average of three minutes to 2 minutes 30 seconds. Fantastic. You're contributing to lower support costs, higher sales, and greater customer satisfaction and loyalty. You're going to get a nice bonus. And if you keep delivering these type of results, you'll be first in line for a promotion."

Linking the TPI with other Key Performance Indicators

One of the weaknesses of customer experience metrics is that in the scale of organizational history, they are a relatively new type of metric for a great many organizations. While an increasing number of managers have bought into the concept of good customer experience, they struggle to understand how improving customer experience actually improves organizational performance.

In such environments, customer experience is potentially endangered because how it drives value is not fully understood. To truly embed a customer experience metric such as Top Tasks within your organization, it is thus vital to link it with more traditional Key Performance Indicators (KPIs). This is not easy to do but it is incredibly essential work. Otherwise, you are likely to find a situation where there is an initial burst of enthusiasm, followed by boredom and a return to old practices. Because let's be crystal clear here: It is much easier for an organization to be organization-centric than to be customer-centric.

What sort of linkages should you be looking for?

- Reduction in support costs that are directly linked to improvement driven by the TPI.
- Increased sales/transactions.
- Channel shift: More people moving from more expensive channels (phone, face-to-face) to digital.
- Increased loyalty: Customers staying longer.

Continuous improvement at Cisco

Troubleshooting is the third most important task for Cisco customers. In November 2012, we measured a troubleshooting task around password recovery:

Pretend you have forgotten the password for the Cisco account and take whatever actions are required to log in.

- It had a 37% failure rate.
- The average time to complete the task was 240 seconds.

When we analyzed the causes of failures and slow times, we found a range of problems. The following screen-grab illustrates just two of the problems:

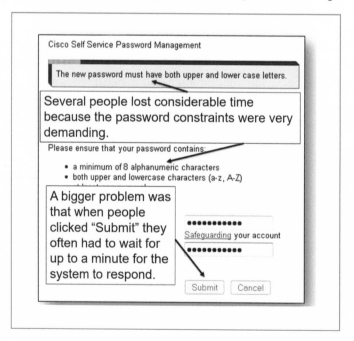

Obviously, improving the speed of the system was the highest priority and this was resolved immediately. They also set about making the inputting of a new password easier.

The next time we ran the TPI in May 2013, the failure rate had dropped by 14% to 23%. Time-on-task had gone from an average of 240 seconds to 215 seconds. Here's how the new password entry screen had been improved.

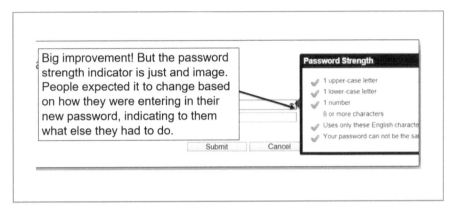

This was definite progress. However, people expected the password strength indicator to be interactive and tell them what conditions they had met, and what conditions were still to meet. "Ah," said the Cisco team, "Good idea! Why didn't we think of that?" Next time we did the TPI in August 2013, here's what it looked like:

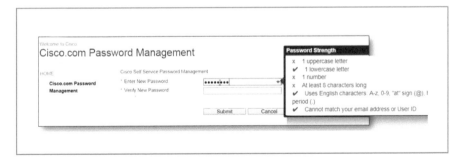

The failure rate had now dropped to 12%. In December 2013, after more tweaking and improvement, it was a 100% success rate. Now, it's quite rare to get a 100% success rate, but Cisco had put together a brilliant, cross-functional, multidisciplinary team. As Martin Hardee, then head of Cisco.com said,

"Implementing the improvements required coordinated effort from multiple IT teams, usability and experience design people, and even content editors."

Job done! Game over?

In March 2014, when we did the next TPI, the success rate had dropped to 59%. A technical error had occurred with the system. It was immediately fixed, and in the July TPI we were back up to a 100% success rate.

Digital is never done. You must keep observing. You must always keep improving. 30 seconds to complete a task today may be seen as fast. In two years' time, it will be seen as too slow.

Digital is never done.

Digital is never done.

Digital is never done.